SPECIAL THANKS

Mike Bondy, Ivan Ponting, Jake Lingwood, Deirdre Owens, BBC Radio Merseyside, *The Kop* magazine (*Liverpool Echo*), Granada Television, London Weekend Television *Up for The Cup*, BBC Radio 5 Live *The House That Bill Built*, BBC Television, Liverpool Daily Post and Echo Ltd, *Sunday Telegraph, Sunday Express, Sunday Mirror, Sunday People, Daily Telegraph, Daily Sketch, Daily Express, The Guardian, Daily Mail, Daily Record* and *Evening Express.*

Previous page:
"It's great to be alive, boys. All you need is the green grass and a football."

First published in Great Britain in 1998

1 3 5 7 9 10 8 6 4 2

© 1998 Steve Hale (photographs) and Phil Thompson (text)

Ebury Press
Random House, 20 Vauxhall Bridge Road, London SW1V 2SA

Random House Australia Pty Limited
20 Alfred Street, milsons Point, Sydney, New South Wales 2061, Australia

Random House New Zealand Limited
18 Poland Road, Glenfield, Auckland 10, New Zealand

Random House South Africa (Pty) Limited
Endulini, 5A Jubilee Road, Parktown 2193, South Africa

Random House UK Limited Reg. No. 954009

A CIP catalogue record for this book is available from the British Library

ISBN 0 09 186453 4

Design by Dan Newman

Printed and bound in Singapore by Tien Wah Press

Papers used by Ebury Press are natural, recyclable products made from wood grown in sustainable forests

THE **SHANKLY** YEARS

A REVOLUTION IN FOOTBALL

Liverpool FC 1959–1974

Steve Hale and Phil Thompson

EBURY
PRESS

CONTENTS

Player Profiles

CHAPTER ONE

1959-61

LIVERPOOL
The Place Where They Live, Eat, Sleep And Drink Football

'We murdered them 0-0.'
Bill Shankly

Bill Shankly was once asked to describe what he found at Liverpool when he arrived in December 1959. His reply was, as ever, blunt and honest: 'Quite candidly, it was a shambles of a place. The team wasn't very good; the ground was run down and wasn't good enough for the team and the supporters.'

But he had played at Anfield many times while a player at Preston and sensed that Liverpool had the capability to be a footballing force. 'I could sense the potential among the crowd. I'd played here and the people were fantastic. They wanted to see their team back in the First Division; they were desperate for success. It was all there waiting to be directed. Liverpool was a city of a million people with a deep love of football. The potential was tremendous and that is why I came to Anfield. I was only interested in one thing, success for the club; which meant success for the people. I wanted to make the people happy.'

As the years unfolded, Shankly did indeed make the people happy. No manager of a football club had ever before, or probably ever will again, have a closer relationship with his club's supporters. It was once quite aptly described as a 'marriage made in

heaven'. 'I'd been at Celtic-Rangers games and seen the fans kissing the team bus. The people are the same kind of people as me. They are passionate about football,' he said.

* * *

That Bill Shankly came to Liverpool in the first place was due largely to club chairman T. V. Williams. Williams, like Shankly, was known as a man of integrity, with much warmth and dignity, and like the tough Scot, he could be short-tempered as well. Williams had spotted something in Shankly when he encountered him over the years. Shankly had actually first applied for the manager's job at Liverpool in the early 1950s, but had failed to get the appointment. Years later

'Like a bolt from the blue came the invitation from Liverpool to join them. Away from prying eyes I signed up as manager in a car in a back street in Manchester one Sunday evening.'
Bill Shankly

Williams persuaded the rest of the Liverpool board that Shankly had the potential to take the club back into the First Division, and after getting assurance from Williams that he would have sole control over team selection, Shankly agreed to take the job.

Prior to Shankly's arrival at the club, successive managers had to have their team selection checked by the boardroom for approval, a situation he couldn't tolerate. He was happy though with the backroom staff already in place at the club, demanding loyalty from them which they eagerly gave, and he returned to them the same loyalty and respect.

Joe Fagan was at the club about a year before the human tornado, Shankly, swept in and recalls, 'We were going nowhere, but the whole club changed when Bill arrived. It started to vibrate. Everything started to move forward for Liverpool. It was his great personality. A beam shone out of him. The other thing about him was that he was a simple

man. There was nothing pretentious about him. Bill Shankly was undoubtedly Liverpool's greatest-ever signing.'

As Joe Fagan says, Shankly did have an incredible ability to appear both magical and ordinary at the same time. Bob Paisley, who during the Shankly years at Anfield held the positions of reserve team trainer, physiotherapist, coach and manager's assistant, before taking over from Shankly and becoming the most successful manager in British football history) also remembered Shankly's arrival at Anfield: 'When Bill came to Liverpool, a friend at Huddersfield told me I'd never be able to work with Bill for more than two years. I wouldn't be able to stand the strain, he said. But from the moment he arrived, we got on like a "house on

Bill Shankly after his arrival at Liverpool in 1959: 'Quite candidly it was a shambles of a place,' he said.

GERRY BYRNE

Liverpool-born Gerry Byrne joined the club in 1955, but it wasn't until Bill Shankly took over as manager in 1959 that his Anfield career began to blossom. Shankly developed Byrne into a full-back who would go on to win international honours. It was hard to believe that this was the same player who was on the transfer list when Shankly arrived, with little interest being shown in him by other clubs. Byrne became a first-team regular in the team that won promotion in 1961-62 and held his place until injuries took their toll in the mid 1960s.

A member of England's 1966 World Cup squad, Byrne will always be remembered for his heroic F A Cup final display against Leeds in 1965. He played 117 minutes of the game with a broken collarbone after Bobby Collins clattered into him. The fact that he managed to conceal the extent of his injury from the Leeds team, and also keep a tight grip on their outstanding winger, Johnny Giles, contributed hugely to Liverpool's victory.

Bob Paisley once described Byrne as, 'A bit of a loner, similar to Kenny Dalglish, in that way. Even though he had little to say, he wouldn't be pushed around on the field. If he got hit he wouldn't forget the bloke who hit him and would soon be after him.'

Gerry Byrne was a key member of Shankly's first great Liverpool team of the mid 1960s, and when the full-back had to retire

prematurely through injury in 1969, Shankly said that a Liverpool team without Byrne in it had something special missing.

fire". Bill was happy with us and we were certainly happy with him. He carried us along through the sheer force of his personality.'

* * *

Shankly's managerial route to Liverpool had been inauspicious, and he had certainly had to learn the hard way about what a demanding job running a

club on a shoe-string budget can be. After periods at Carlisle, Grimsby and Workington, he finally moved up the football ladder as assistant to first-team boss Andy Beattie at Huddersfield, a club with a great history but who were struggling, unsuccessfully as it turned out, to avoid relegation to the Second Division. Eventually, Shankly took over

Opposite: Bill Shankly hands out a few tips to Ronnie Moran. When asked about Shankly's impact on the club, Moran replied, 'I learned more in the first three months than I'd done in the seven years I'd been a pro. I just wish I'd been five years younger.'

Dave Hickson puts in a header against Derby County at Anfield in 1960.

from Beattie as first-team manager, but was unsuccessful in his attempt to get Huddersfield back in to the top flight.

After taking over at Liverpool, Shankly faced initially the same major dilemma as he had done at Huddersfield: it was no good having ambition without ammunition, and he needed money to buy players. It was as simple as that, and unsuccessful bids were made to bring Jack Charlton and Scottish midfield dynamo, Dave Mackay, to the club. Shankly had been told by the Liverpool board when he had taken the manager's job that they were as ambitious for success as he was, but during his early period at the club, he began to doubt this. The question started to play on Shankly's mind: should he have stayed at Huddersfield Town?

Anfield and the club's training ground at Melwood were also of a very poor standard for a club that was supposedly ambitious. Bill's wife, Nessie, was happy at Huddersfield and admits that during their early days on Merseyside, there was much soul-searching being done by her husband. 'The Liverpool people couldn't have been warmer

or more welcoming,' she says. 'The club, however, was a big disappointment to Bill. The biggest shock of all to him was the training ground at Melwood. I remember we were standing in the middle of the pitch at Melwood and Bill said to me, "Oh Ness, have I made a terrible mistake leaving Huddersfield?" He thought at that moment that coming to Liverpool was a big mistake because the conditions at the training ground were so appalling.

'Nobody would believe it. Bill had a battle on his hands. He would go there every day with Bob Paisley, Reuben Bennett, Joe Fagan and the groundsman at Melwood, Eli Wass, and they were digging up the place with their bare hands. There were bricks and stones everywhere. All there was was a dirty little hut where the players changed. There was no running water. Anfield wasn't much better. It was a nice ground, but rather dilapidated at that time. There was no water supply for the pitch, so they had to get cracking on that, get in touch with the council and get a water supply into the ground. It all took a long time.'

* * *

JIMMY MELIA

Local boy Jimmy Melia joined the club as a fifteen-year-old in 1955. He scored on his debut against Nottingham Forest and Shankly regarded him as a vital member of the team that would attempt to achieve his objective of gaining promotion to the First Division.
In the top flight, Melia's undoubted talents were soon recognised by the England selectors and two international caps were awarded to him in 1963.

Although he never retained the goal-scoring ratio that he achieved in the Second Division, Melia looked to be playing a major part in Liverpool's Championship-winning campaign of 1963-64, but an injury at a crucial time in the season saw Shankly introduce Alf Arrowsmith into the side in place of him. Ian St John was withdrawn into a deeper role and these tactics were such a success that Melia had difficulty regaining his place when he was fit again. This was often the case at Liverpool during this period, with many players admitting that they often played carrying injuries, rather than tell Shankly they were unfit. 'Once you lost your place, someone may move in and take it for good' was the general fear expressed by the Liverpool players of this era.

Jimmy Melia didn't regain his place in the Liverpool team and signed for Wolves for £55,000 in 1964.

The great Billy Liddell was coming to the end of his career when Shankly arrived. During the 1950s Liverpool was known as 'Liddellpool', and a fan once expressed the sentiments of many when he said, 'Before Shankly all we had to be proud of was Billy Liddell. A few years later we had a whole team to be proud of.'

of months, I knew who I thought could play and who couldn't. That was my first priority at Anfield, to get to know the people I was working with. I had to assess the whole place, the directors as well.'

His assessment of the club's directors left him with the uncomfortable feeling that obtaining financial backing to bring in new blood was going to be a struggle.

He once declared: 'At a football club, there's a holy trinity; the players, the manager and the supporters. Directors don't come into it. They are only there to sign the cheques; not to make them out. We'll do that, they just sign them.'

* * *

Shankly's first full season at the club, 1960-61, saw them once again finish in third spot. He was now desperate for someone in a position of authority at the club to 'sign the cheques'. Fortunately for Shankly, that man had now arrived.

'Eric Sawyer was the beginning of Liverpool,' Shankly claimed. 'He was willing to spend money. He said to me, "If you can get the players, I'll get you the money".'

Sawyer, an accountant and key figure in charge of finance at the Littlewoods Pools organisation, was placed on the board at Liverpool at the behest of Littlewoods' founding figure, John Moores. Moores was now chairman at Everton and, after pumping substantial amounts of money into the club, was about to preside over the re-emergence of Everton as a force in British football. Moores also had substantial shares in Liverpool Football Club and this entitled him to place a nominee on the board at Anfield – that man was Eric Sawyer. Sawyer, unlike the majority of directors that Shankly had had to deal with in his football career, wasn't interested in telling him who should or shouldn't be in the team.

The Liverpool boss could now spend the summer months of 1961 plotting Liverpool's all-out push for promotion in a more optimistic frame of mind. But he still had to face the wrath of the shareholders before the new season began. ●

On the playing side, the arrival of Shankly at Liverpool resulted in them putting in a spirited effort to catch the clubs chasing a promotion spot, although they could only finish in third place. There was now, however, a buzz about the club, and Liverpool's captain at the time, Ronnie Moran, who has served the club with distinction and loyalty as both a player and member of the backroom staff since the beginning of the Shankly years, once explained: 'I learned more in the first three months than I'd done in the seven years that I'd been a pro. I wish I'd been five years younger.' Shankly used that first season at the club to assess the players he had at his disposal. 'After a couple

CHAPTER TWO

1961-62

PROMOTION OR BUST
Could Mr Shankly Explain Why His Team Are Not Trying?

'Call me a fanatic if you like, but I never asked for a contract. I had none in those days and I haven't got one now. I told the board, "If I don't like you I will be free to go. If you don't like me you can send me packing." My sentiments are unchanged.'
Bill Shankly, 1962

To accuse **Bill Shankly** of instructing his players not to try during a game of football is akin to suggesting that George Best has been celibate for the past thirty years. But incredibly, this accusation was put to the Liverpool manager during a heated post-mortem after another disappointing season at Anfield. Liverpool's failure to gain promotion in 1961 led to ructions at the club's annual meeting of shareholders. Both the chairman, T. V. Williams, and Shankly came under heavy criticism from an irate group of shareholders, who demanded to know why the team had finished as Second Division also-rans yet again:

'Tell me, Mr Shankly,' enquired Solly Isenwater, who was chairman of the Shareholders Association, 'is it true that you have ever said that when the team were leading by one or two clear goals, they could take it easy, and not get injured?'

A seething Shankly got to his feet and replied, 'That's rubbish. I have never heard anything so

Bill Shankly attends a
dinner with Billy Liddell,
chairman T. V. Williams
and the Lord Mayor of
Liverpool in 1961.

silly.' Fighting hard to keep his anger under control, he went on, 'I think the tension on players is too much for them to carry. It's not created by one or two failures to gain promotion, but by the past seven seasons.'

Not satisfied by his reply, one of the shareholders expressed the view that some of the players were just not good enough and that money must be spent to bring in new talent. T. V. Williams told the meeting that the directors were making continuous efforts to obtain players and could have spent millions if Liverpool's bids had been accepted. 'Players are refusing to come to Liverpool. We've been up and down the country, day and night, looking for players, but they preferred London where they still thought the streets were paved with gold,' he said.

'Is Goodison Park in London, because they seem to get the players all right,' another unhappy shareholder sarcastically responded.

Returning to the point made earlier in the meeting about Liverpool players' lack of effort, Solly Isenwater remarked, 'The board should have taken action to show supporters that no Liverpool player could just stop playing in the middle of a game. Certainly no member of the board, or any businessman, would allow an employee to stop work as and when he pleased.'

Williams reiterated Shankly's reply to this question and informed Isenwater that he was 'talking a lot of nonsense'. 'And in any case, why should you know?' the short-tempered chairman responded. This brought an angry response from many of the shareholders and a proposed vote of no confidence in the chair was averted only after a period of cooling down.

* * *

One thing was made patently obvious to Shankly, who must have been absolutely livid at the mere suggestion that he would ever send a team out to play who would ever give anything less than 100 per cent effort, was that if his gamble in spending what at the time were huge fees to bring in Ian St John and Ron Yeats failed, and Liverpool didn't win promotion, then his rejuvenating of Liverpool may

have ended before he had even set the wheels fully in motion. Clearly the shareholders were now as impatient for success as Shankly was himself.

It's also worth bearing in mind that attendance figures at Anfield had dropped from an average of 38,000 before Shankly arrived, to below the 30,000 mark for the first time since the pre-war years. This was another key factor in the shareholders' concern over Liverpool's continuation as an under-achieving Second Division side.

It has been documented that during the early 1960s, Shankly came very close to resigning as Liverpool manager and that it was only his close friend Sir Matt Busby who persuaded him to persevere at Liverpool. It was probably after attending the shareholders' angry annual meeting in 1961 that Shankly came near to terminating his managership of the club. Chairman Williams ended the stormy meeting by reminding them that just a few weeks previously, Scottish international Ian St John had joined the club for a £35,000 fee, and he pledged that 'within the limits of common sense and sound business dealing, the board would do everything possible to bring about the club's return to the First Division'. Williams concluded by stating, 'When we meet here next year, on the occasion of the 70th annual meeting, I hope we will have achieved our objective, which unfortunately has eluded us much too long.'

* * *

The signing of Ian St John was to prove crucial in Liverpool's drive towards First Division status. Shankly had been alerted to his possible availability after reading of the player's discontent at Motherwell in the *Sunday Post*. Once given the green light by the board that the money would be made available to sign the talented Scot, Shankly travelled up to see him with director S. C. Reakes, arriving in time to watch St John play for Motherwell against Hamilton Academicals in the Lanarkshire Cup. St John scored and an impressed director Reakes was only too happy to open negotiations for his transfer at the end of the game. Newcastle were also interested in him, but after

continued on page 20

ROGER HUNT

Roger Hunt, from Lancashire, was the idol of the Kop in the 1960s where he was dubbed 'Sir Roger'. Hunt turned professional with Liverpool after completing his National Service and made his debut against Scunthorpe in 1959. He was soon amongst the goals and went on to score 285 for the club before leaving in 1969.

Apart from his ability to score on a regular basis, Hunt's work-rate was phenomenal and it was because of this unselfish side to his game that Sir Alf Ramsey gave him the vote over the brilliant goal poacher, Jimmy Greaves, in the 1966 World Cup.

'He didn't have the individual skills of Greavsie, but he would run, and run, all day. He ran himself into the ground as the workhorse in that World-Cup-winning side,' Bob Paisley once said of Hunt's contribution to England's victory.

1966 was, in fact, probably the highlight of Hunt's career, with a World Cup winners' medal, a Championship medal, and European Cup Winners' Cup losers' medal all coming his way.

He continued to knock in the goals for Liverpool until the late 1960s, when he signed for Bolton. His Anfield team-mate throughout this period, Ian Callaghan, said, 'It's little wonder that the Kop dubbed him "Sir Roger", for although he took so much stick up front, he took it all in his stride, never retaliated and got on with the business in hand … scoring.'

THE SECOND DIVISION
21 April 1962

Liverpool	**2**
Southampton	**0**

Considering that summer was nearly here, this game was played in almost freak conditions. A constant downpour and grey atmosphere meant that Anfield was shrouded in such a cloud of darkness, that by mid-afternoon, the floodlights had to be switched on. Despite the conditions, Liverpool's rain-sodden fans were in heaven by the time the final whistle had blown. Liverpool were back in the First Division.

The atrocious weather kept the attendance down to 40,000, when over 50,000 had been expected to cram into Anfield to witness Liverpool's expected return to the top flight. Both Liverpool and Southampton made light of the appalling conditions to produce an excellent first half, with each team attacking from the start.

Liverpool had goalkeeper Jim Furnell to thank for keeping them in the game with a string of outstanding saves. Kevin Lewis, playing as centre forward in place of the injured St John, opened the scoring for Liverpool. After a scramble in the Southampton goalmouth, the ball fell to Lewis who managed to divert it into the net. Southampton hit back immediately when Terry Paine centred to Clifton, whose header beat Furnell only to see the ball hit a Liverpool post before falling to safety. Five minutes later, in the 30th minute, Lewis scored Liverpool's second. Southampton goalkeeper Godfrey could only palm away a Callaghan centre and Lewis pounced to head the ball into the goal. The Anfield crowd went berserk, Bill Shankly's promise to take Liverpool back into the First Division had almost been fulfilled.

In the second half, the weather conditions continued to deteriorate, and although Southampton pressed to get back into the game, Liverpool's lead never really looked in danger. The pitch had now become such a bog that both sides were finding it difficult to keep their feet.

The scenes that greeted the final whistle hadn't been witnessed at Anfield for many a year. The Southampton team formed a guard of honour and applauded the Liverpool team from the pitch. The crowd chanted for their heroes and eventually, they emerged from their dressing room. Ron Yeats and Ian St John, key figures in Liverpool's glorious season, were engulfed by fans in scenes of mass hysteria. Yeats, after being pushed over a boundary wall by fans wanting to pat him on the back, or shake his hand, escaped back to the safety of the dressing rooms. Ian St John wasn't so lucky, and after being hoisted on to the shoulders of well-wishers, was carried off into the mass of the supporters. Luckily, police came to the young Scot's rescue and got him back to the sanctuary of the dressing room.

Chairman T. V. Williams told the supporters, 'The hardest thing in football is to win the Second Division championship. There are forty-two cup-ties to contend with. Next year, we hope we will be top of the First Division.'

Bill Shankly said this was his happiest moment in football: 'We won the title in the first month of the season, when we were fitter than our rivals. We beat Sunderland and Newcastle twice in that spell and we never looked back. We have a great team and they are still young. Most of them are only boys. Talented boys, sure, but still only boys. I believe Liverpool are on the threshold of great things.' He then paid tribute to his back-room team, 'I was disappointed, on arrival, at many things I found at Anfield, but my training and coaching staff have never given me a moment's anxiety. We have worked perfectly together and in Messrs Bennett, Paisley, Shelley and Fagan, I have a real team behind a team.'

As ever, his final word of praise was for his beloved Liverpool supporters. 'Of course I'm delighted that Liverpool are back in the First Division, where they belong and where they have always belonged. But one of the greatest thrills I capture from it all is the knowledge that our wonderful supporters have seen the accomplishment of their ambition. Without their intense loyalty, how much harder it would have been for each one of us! Now they have a team worthy of them and that is how it must be kept.'

Liverpool: Furnell, Byrne, Moran, Milne, Yeats, Leishman, Callaghan, Hunt, Lewis, Melia, A'Court

Southampton: Godfrey, Patrick, Traynor, Wilmshurst, Knapp, Huxford, Paine, Clifton, Reeves, Mulgrew, Penk

Jubilant Liverpool players after their 1962 promotion-winning victory over Southampton.

GORDON MILNE

Gordon Milne was Bill Shankly's first major signing when he paid Preston £16,000 to bring him to Anfield in 1960. Milne took a little time to adjust to his new club, but when he did, he gave Liverpool tremendous service. After helping Liverpool win promotion, he took to the First Division scene well, and went on to win fourteen England caps during the 1963-64 period. There was heartbreak for Milne, however, in the 1965 F A Cup final, with injury keeping him out of the game. Milne, an industrious worker in midfield, was never a headline maker, but was invaluable in the engine room of Shankly's outstanding 1960s team.

He went on to make 277 appearances for Liverpool before signing for Blackpool in 1967. His best playing years were now behind him and in 1970 he became player-manager at Wigan before taking over the managerial reins at Coventry.

continued from page 16

Shankly had worked hard at selling Liverpool to St John, his destination was only ever going to be Anfield.

St John quickly became a firm favourite with the Liverpool supporters, and in the mid 1960s, the story about the church sign in the city centre that posed the question 'What will you do when Christ comes to lead us again?', which had the response scribbled underneath by one of the Anfield brethren 'Move St John to inside-forward', was re-told over and over again.

Shankly's next acquisition during the summer of 1961 was the Dundee United centre-half Ron Yeats. Initially Shankly had wanted to bring Jack Charlton from Leeds, but couldn't convince the board that Charlton was worth the money Leeds were asking. Shankly's search for a centre-half led him to Yeats and, after initially being rebuffed by Dundee, Shankly persuaded the Liverpool board to part with £30,000 for the Scot who would prove to be the foundation that much of Liverpool's success in the 1960s would be built on.

Interviewed in later years, Yeats said he couldn't resist signing for Shankly after spending just a short period of time in the company of the indomitable Liverpool manager. 'I asked him, "Whereabouts in England is Liverpool?"' recalled Yeats, meaning where about in the country was Liverpool. '"Oh, we're in the First Division, son," replied Shanks. This took me aback, I said, "I thought you were in the Second Division?" Quick as a flash, Shankly replied, "When we sign you, we'll be in the First Division next year." How could I fail to sign for someone who had so much faith in me. Shanks was an amazing man, he really was.'

Shankly himself acknowledged that the arrival of St John and Yeats did more for Liverpool's rise from the Second Division to the First than any other factor. 'Yeats could have played in the Second Division on his own with no other defenders with him and won it,' Shankly was later to claim.

Within months of his arrival, Yeats was appointed team captain, Shankly telling the 6ft 2in Scot, whom he had nicknamed his 'Red Colossus', 'Christ son! You're so big that when you lead the team out, you'll frighten the opposition to death.'

With Yeats and St John supplementing the squad, Shankly now believed that he had a team that fulfilled the wishes of both the board and the disenchanted Liverpool supporters. With the new season just days away, Shankly told Tom Williams, Eric Sawyer and any other board members that came his way that this Liverpool team would not only win promotion, but also the much coveted F A Cup, the trophy that Liverpool had never before won. But although Shankly may have been confident outwardly about Liverpool's prospects in the coming season, he knew that this was make or break time, so he decided to increase the chances of success on the field of play by taking the then revolutionary step of having their opponents checked on by either himself or a member of staff before every game. He was clearly taking no chances, as another season without promotion would have been a catastrophe.

* * *

Liverpool's opening game was at Bristol Rovers and resulted in a comfortable 2-0 victory. A few days later, just under 50,000 packed into Anfield to see

Liverpool take on the team that many thought would be one of Liverpool's main rivals for promotion, Sunderland. Two goals from Hunt and another from Lewis gave Liverpool another easy win. Leeds and Sunderland away were next on the list and Liverpool knocked in nine more goals to maintain their fantastic start to the season.

Liverpool didn't taste their first defeat until mid October and the promotion that everyone at Anfield had craved for so long looked to be a foregone conclusion. Their attack was knocking in goals for fun, with the Yeats-led defence proving as mean as Shankly had suspected it would be once Yeats was in the line-up.

Promotion was clinched on 21 April 1962 against Southampton at Anfield, when a crowd of over 40,000 witnessed their 2-0 victory, both goals coming from Kevin Lewis. Everyone at Anfield was ecstatic – Liverpool had had little to celebrate since the team of Stubbins and company had won the championship in 1947, and everyone intended to make up for lost time. The players were lost in a sea of celebrating fans as they chanted their heroes' names. The Kop wanted to savour this moment of triumph and wouldn't allow the team to disappear to their dressing room. They refused to leave the ground and chanted 'Liv-er-pool, Liv-er-pool' incessantly.

The moment that Shankly had dreamed of since he had moved into football management had arrived. He was leading a football club who were now the size of an army. Right from the start of his managerial career, it was Shankly's aim to harness both the team and the supporters into one. To him, football was a communal experience; the team was an extension of the fans on the pitch and the fans an extension of the team on the terraces. Shankly knew from his playing days the type of passion and noise that the Kop and the rest of Anfield was capable of. Now it had reached full fruition and although it frightened even some of the Liverpool players on that momentous spring day in 1962, it would be used to even greater effect to terrify Liverpool's opponents in the years that would follow.

The success of Liverpool added an even greater buzz to a city that was teetering on the brink of a musical explosion in the early 1960s. There were also now two First Division teams to be proud of, and buoyed by their team's success, an application was made by Liverpool to the Liverpool City Council to have the city's coat of arms displayed on the players' shirts. They cited the fact that Bolton, Nottingham Forest, Newcastle and other famous clubs had their city's coat of arms displayed on their teams shirts. 'Our present badge contains only the Liver Bird,' stated a representative of the board. 'Surely we could do more for the city of Liverpool by showing the badge abroad and elsewhere in Britain.' It was all to no avail and Liverpool's request to replace the Liver Bird that would become so symbolic with Liverpool's success in years to come was turned down by the City council.

After winning promotion against Southampton, Liverpool entertained Stoke City at Anfield two days later. A crowd of over 41,000 saw goals by Moran and Jimmy Melia give Liverpool a narrow 2-1 victory over Stoke.

The following morning, club secretary, James McInnes, arrived at Anfield to discover that safe-blowers had forced their way into the club's office and blown open a safe containing all of the previous evening's takings of more than £4,000 and most of the championship medals that had been deposited there for safe keeping. Liverpool acted quickly in contacting the Football League to obtain replacements for the stolen medals. But the gloss of finally winning promotion had been slightly eroded by the Anfield intruders. ●

Liverpool captain Ron Yeats is presented with the Second Division trophy in 1962.

CHAPTER THREE

1962-63

MIND OVER MATTER
Success Is In Your Head,
As Well As Your Feet

'All players are born.
Anyone who tells you that
they can make players
are very stupid people.'
Bill Shankly

Liverpool began the 1962-63 season, their first season in Division One since 1954, in an unconvincing way. An attendance of 51,000 crammed into Anfield to see them play Lancashire rivals Blackpool, and Blackpool took the points with a 2-1 victory. An away trip to Manchester City followed by a home game against Blackburn also failed to see Liverpool register a victory.

Shankly put down Liverpool's tentative start to giving too much respect to the opposition. After some hard-hitting team talks, during which Shankly would display his growing expertise at the psychological side of football management, Liverpool's result began to improve. He motivated his team by eulogising about what a wonderful group of players they were, and what rubbish most of the so-called First Division élite were. All of Liverpool's opponents came in for the Shankly treatment, particularly the London clubs – Spurs were nicknamed by Shankly 'the Drury Lane fan dancers' and outstanding Tottenham players such as Dave Mackay, who Shankly had practically

Roger Hunt equalises against Everton in the final minute to give Liverpool a 2-2 draw in 1962.

Roger Hunt and Ian St John try on new Gola footwear; multi-million-pound endorsement deals were still a thing of the future, but players did get a free pair of boots.

praise a Leeds player, Shankly would just say 'a fair player, nae bad', leaving Revie wondering how his team ever won a game.

* * *

Liverpool's results did begin to improve and wins against Manchester City, Sheffield United and West Ham put the team in good heart for the first Merseyside derby for nearly ten years. City rivals Everton were among the favourites to take the League title and were fancied by most neutrals to put one over on Shankly's First Division new boys. 73,000 packed into Goodison Park for the eagerly awaited contest, and it was Everton who took first blood with a penalty scored by captain Roy Vernon. Lewis equalised for Liverpool before half-time, followed by another for Everton by Johnny Morrisey in the second half. Most of those present thought the points were in the bag for the blue half of Merseyside. With 90 minutes up on the clock, Liverpool were pressing hard for an equaliser, and winger Alan A'Court dispatched one last cross into the Everton penalty area. Up popped Roger Hunt to evade the challenges of Gordon West and Brian Labone to smack the ball into the Everton net.

It was always a feature of Liverpool's play throughout the Shankly years that they fought and fought until the final whistle, and this, like on many other occasions in the future, was one of the games when this philosophy brought its rewards. The Liverpudlians in Goodison erupted as the referee blew for full-time within seconds of the Hunt goal that meant so much to their team's standing on Merseyside. Recalling his equaliser years later Hunt remarked, 'The Merseyside derby means so much to so many people. If we had lost, then our supporters would have had to wait six months for a chance of revenge, so to score such an important late goal was an indescribable feeling for me.'

After the game, arguments raged between Everton and Liverpool fans about whether the referee should have blown for time before Hunt's equaliser and should Everton have been awarded a penalty in the first half. But generally, these disagreements were good-natured banter that rarely

begged the Liverpool board to sign when Mackay was still a Hearts player, were branded as over-the-hill and past it.

The idiosyncratic Liverpool boss didn't really believe it, and neither did the majority of his players, but somehow Shankly's rubbishing of the opposition did begin to give his Liverpool players a psychological advantage. Arsenal, West Ham ('a bunch of playboys', including the great Bobby Moore) and every other London club were labelled by Shankly as 'soft southerners'. Practically every First Division team was given the Shankly treatment.

Don Revie, who was in the process of creating a Leeds United team that would become Liverpool's major rivals for honours over the next ten seasons, would receive a regular Sunday-morning call from Shankly, who would praise every member of his Liverpool team one by one; no player had a weakness. If Revie managed to get a word in to

IAN ST JOHN

Bill Shankly once said, 'The arrival of Ian St John and Ronnie Yeats was the very beginning of Liverpool's rise. They did more for the rise than anyone else.'

'The Saint', as he became known, was signed from Motherwell at the end of the 1960-61 season. He was a record buy for Liverpool at £35,000, and was an immediate sensation, scoring a hat-trick against Everton in the Liverpool Senior Cup. Although a little on the small side for a striker at just 5ft 7ins, he made up for his lack of height with his skill, courage and tenacity. He immediately struck up an outstanding partnership with Roger Hunt and the goals flowed.

St John had an outstanding footballing brain, and even when Shankly was forced to move him into a deeper role during the Championship season of 1963-64, St John quickly adapted to what his boss wanted from him. The arrival of St John at Anfield helped to bring on Roger Hunt and, working in tandem, they created a double-act that put many a defence to the sword.

St John won 21 Scottish international caps and will best be remembered as the scorer of the winning goal in the 1965 F A Cup final. He made over 400 appearances for Liverpool, scoring 118 goals. He left Liverpool to join Coventry in 1971, his place in Anfield folklore firmly established.

boiled over into anything physical. Football commentators have remarked many times in the years preceding this first Merseyside derby of the 1960s about the uniqueness of Everton and Liverpool fans walking to the game together and standing (nowadays sitting) side by side during the 90 minutes with little hint of trouble, but this was the first time it had been seen in action by television and the media in general. It was a phenomenon Bill Shankly also found unique and he commented on this during the 1970s: 'The rivalry between Everton and Liverpool is like Celtic and Rangers without the bigotry. There are families in Liverpool with two supporting Everton and two supporting Liverpool. I've never seen a fight at a derby game. This is unusual. They are the same people really.'

* * *

Despite the confidence booster of the derby draw, Shankly knew that new blood was needed to boost his squad. When he heard that classy Rangers half-back Willie Stevenson was unable to gain a regular

Ian St John scores a brilliant goal in Liverpool's 1962 3-3 draw against Manchester United.

first-team place at the Glasgow club, he acted quickly to rescue the Scot from Australian football where he was languishing on loan. A £20,000 fee brought Stevenson to Anfield in October 1962. Photographer Barry Farrell was sent to Anfield to cover the arrival of Stephenson at Liverpool and recalls an incident that displayed how Shankly stamped his mark on a new arrival straight away, 'Negotiations were completed and Shanks was showing Willie around Anfield. One incident sticks in my memory. Shanks stepped out of a car with Willie and they were about to enter the players' entrance. There was a small group of wide-eyed Liverpool kids waiting by the entrance, pens at the ready, hoping to obtain the autographs of any of their heroes who might happen to pass by. Willie went to walk into the entrance when Shanks exclaimed, "Willie, son! You've forgotten something." Liverpool's latest acquisition looked bemused as he wondered what his new boss was talking about. "You've forgotten something, son,"

Shanks repeated. Willie was still none the wiser. "Willie, son, go and sign the children's books," Shanks quietly ordered. Willie looked relieved and was only too happy to comply with his manager's wishes. It may appear to be an insignificant incident, but it gives an example of how Shankly was eager to display to a new signing that the Anfield brethren, whether young or old, come first.'

Although Stevenson took a little time to settle, once he did he became a key figure in Shankly's team. His passing skills were first class and together with Milne and Jimmy Melia, he became a key member of the Liverpool team that would storm to the League title in such thrilling fashion the following season. Willie was also a joker around the dressing room and helped to create the kind of atmosphere that successful teams thrive under.

Shankly also introduced goalkeeper Tommy Lawrence into the team during the same period of Stevenson's introduction and this much underrated keeper would, like Stephenson, become a key

element of Shankly's first great team. The brave Lawrence, who was adept at diving at the feet of opposing forwards bearing in on goal, would also go on to win Scottish international honours.

* * *

Boosted by the motivational skills of Shankly and the injection of new blood into the team, Liverpool's results did begin to pick up, and during the November to February period they ran up a sequence of nine consecutive victories.

The rest of the First Division now began to realise that Shankly's passionate orations about his outstanding Liverpool team were no longer an idle boast. Liverpool's dramatic improvement in form coincided with one of the worst winters in living memory, with the big freeze leading to the cancellation of many fixtures. It was during the early weeks of January 1963 that most of the country was in the grip of arctic conditions and Shankly was desperate to give his team some much-needed match practice. He contacted Everton manager Harry Catterick and asked him did he fancy taking on his Liverpool team behind closed doors at Everton's training ground at Bellefield. Harry agreed and the game took place on a snow-covered pitch. After the game, which Liverpool lost, Shankly was heard to exclaim, tongue-in-cheek, 'That bloody referee is a disgrace. He shouldn't have allowed that game to take place. The pitch wasn't safe.'

Although Liverpool couldn't maintain their outstanding League form when League football returned once pitches became playable again, hopes were high that this was going to be the year that they would win the FA Cup for the very first time.

After defeating Wrexham 3-0, they were drawn to play Burnley at Turf Moor. At the time, Burnley were a strong First Division outfit and a 1-1 draw in the first game brought the Lancashire side back to Anfield for the replay. A pitch inspection was needed to allow the game to take place. Shankly, vigilant as ever, watched the referee make his way out on to the frosty Anfield turf and then spotted that Burnley manager Harry Potts was also walking out on to the pitch. Shankly had never had much

time for the then Burnley Chairman, Bob Lord, an outspoken Lancastrian businessman, and seized on the opportunity to take a swipe at Burnley through their manager Harry Potts. 'Hey you, Potts!' he shouted to the startled Burnley manager. 'Get off our pitch. You don't find me walking all over your pitch at Turf Moor. Get off it, now!' The bemused Burnley boss left the referee to make the inspection on his own and the match was given the go-ahead. After extra-time, Liverpool won the replay and went on to defeat Arsenal and West Ham on their way to a semi-final tie against Leicester. 65,000 attended the game, held at Hillsborough, but despite continuous pressure, Leicester ran off 1-0 winners. Gordon Banks, later regarded as the best goalkeeper in the world, was outstanding as Leicester put up the type of rearguard action that had become their trademark. It was Leicester's third victory over Liverpool that season and Shankly had no doubts that they had had their Wembley dream ended by the best team in the League.

* * *

Many of the Liverpool team, several of whom would go on to win major honours in the next few seasons, regarded the Leicester defeat as the most disappointing moment of their Anfield career. It was rather odd, in fact, that Shankly would go on to acclaim Leicester as the top team of the season. Leicester were renowned for their defensive capabilities, and a style of play that the attack-minded Shankly would usually have been adverse to in the extreme. But perhaps the fact that 'that lot across the park', Everton, had just been crowned League champions, playing an attractive style of attacking play that usually would have had Shankly drooling, may have had something to do with his declarations on who were currently the best team in the League.

Although Liverpool's first season back in the First Division ended in disappointing fashion, losing six of their last nine games, including a 7-2 defeat at the hands of 'the Drury Lane fan dancers' – Spurs – Shankly was confident that they could more than hold their own; the new season couldn't come soon enough for the enthusiastic Scot. ●

F A CUP SEMI-FINAL
27 April 1963

Liverpool	**0**
Leicester	**1**

An indignant Bill Shankly described this result in a bitter post-match summary as, 'A travesty of a result. It was the most one-sided game I have ever seen. Even the Leicester supporters were too stunned to cheer.'

The omens didn't look good from the start for Liverpool, with Jimmy Melia, the one player who may have unlocked the well-drilled Leicester defence, being declared unfit with an ankle injury. Liverpool brought in youngster Chris Lawler to play in defence, with Gordon Milne taking Melia's role in midfield.

The pattern of the game was set from the opening minutes, with Liverpool attacking from the start and Leicester content to soak up the pressure and hoping to hit Liverpool on the break. With Gordon Banks in the Leicester goal in outstanding form, Leicester rode their luck and took the lead after only 18 minutes, when Mike Stringfellow latched on to a Riley free kick and glanced a header past Tommy Lawrence. Leicester's 'smash and grab' tactics had brought them early success.

After that it was practically all one-way traffic, as Liverpool bombarded the Leicester goal for an equaliser. Leicester's defensive style of play had brought them much success during the season, and today was the day when Liverpool found out just what a tough nut they were to crack. The ball was lofted into the Leicester goalmouth time and time again, but the breakthrough just wouldn't come for the Liverpool team, who were badly missing the guile of Melia.

If the first half had been 80 per cent Liverpool pressure, the second half was practically 100 per cent Liverpool bombardment of the Leicester goal. Even centre-half, Ron Yeats, went into attack as Liverpool pressed relentlessly for a goal. Tackles became fiercer and more rugged as the tension mounted, and Sjoberg of Leicester was booked. Roger Hunt thought he had put Liverpool on level terms when he placed

Chris Lawler, who was brought in to replace the injured Jimmy Melia.

a shot to the left of Banks, but the acrobatic keeper leapt to his side and clutched the ball with his fingertips on the line. Hunt then sent in a header that defeated Banks, but the ball crashed against the bar before being booted to safety.

Near the end, the Leicester team looked weary and about to crack at any moment, but from somewhere, they drew on extra reserves of stamina to hold on for a famous victory. They had placed their faith entirely in defensive play and had won the day. Ian St John, who had ran himself into a frenzy in Liverpool's cause, was practically in tears as he trooped off the pitch with his similarly dejected Liverpool team-mates. The magnificent Gordon Banks, who had done so much to take his team to Wembley, was a picture of happiness as he celebrated with the Leicester team.

Leicester manager, Matt Gillies, said he was happy with the result but not with the way Leicester played. 'I felt that one goal would settle this match. I wasn't too happy about the way we achieved our victory, but I'm sure you will see the real Leicester at Wembley.'

Bill Shankly blamed the heavy Hillsborough pitch for Liverpool's downfall and the goal that defeated them. 'Had the Hillsborough pitch been dry, and the ball bouncing, that goal could never have happened,' he commented. The injured Jimmy Melia said his team couldn't have tried harder, 'Nobody could have done more than those lads and nobody was more deserving of victory.'

Liverpool: Lawrence, Byrne, Moran, Milne, Yeats, Stevenson, Callaghan, Hunt, St John, Lawler, Lewis

Leicester City: Banks, Sjoberg, Norman, McLintock, King, Appleton, Riley, Cross, Keyworth, Gibson, Stringfellow

RON YEATS

'Ronnie Yeats could have played in the Second Division with no other defenders with him and still won it!', Bill Shankly once exclaimed. After the Liverpool boss had coaxed the giant Dundee United player to sign for him in 1961, he was confident that promotion was a formality.

The stories about Shankly inviting the press into the showers at Anfield to 'take a walk around his new signing' are true. 'This man is a Colossus,' Shankly told the press, and at 6ft 2in and 14½ stone, he wasn't exaggerating.

Shankly believed that any great team had to be built down the middle: a solid goal-keeper, outstanding striker and a rock-hard centre-half. With Yeats, St John and later Tommy Lawrence, Liverpool had the foundations in place to aim for the top. Shankly actually spotted Yeats while checking out Ian St John in a Scotland Under-23 international. Yeats was playing for the Army team against the Scottish team, and Shankly immediately pencilled in the name of the young Aberdeen-born player in his notebook.

Yeats went on to win international honours himself and has accurately been described as the foundation on which much of the Shankly revolution at Anfield was built. Yeats's heading power, tackling and footballing brain were all first-class, and Shankly lost little time in appointing him club captain. Yeats was also capable of scoring vital goals, and with his considerable height and heading ability was always a source of danger in the opposition's penalty area. Quietly spoken and affable off the pitch, he was the perfect ambassador for the club on their early European adventures.

After 450 appearances for Liverpool, Yeats lost his place to Larry Lloyd and decided to take up an offer to manage Tranmere Rovers in 1971.

'He was brave, a tremendous skipper, a good example to all the young lads at the club and he never allowed himself to get a carried away with his own success,' was how Bob Paisley summed up Ron Yeats.

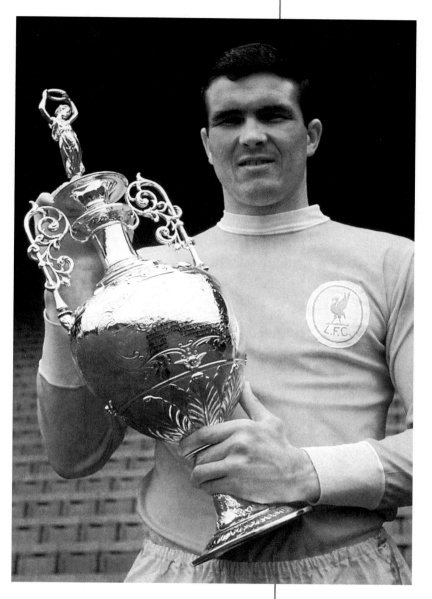

Ron Yeats holds the 1964 League Championship trophy.

CHAPTER FOUR

1963-64

CHAMPIONS
We Love You, Yeah, Yeah, Yeah

'What am I on here ...
a bloody commando course?'
Geoff Strong, after his first day's training at Liverpool

Towards the end of the 1962-63 season, Shankly signed a player from his former club, Preston, who would become a crowd-pleaser at Anfield for the rest of the decade.

Peter Thompson was what Shankly would describe as a 'twisty-turny' player who reminded the Liverpool boss of the player whom he regarded as 'the star of all the stars', Tom Finney. Together with Ian Callaghan, Thompson would terrorise First Division full-backs in the coming season.

Shankly was supremely optimistic before the beginning of the 1963-64 season and told the Liverpool shareholders that he would bring the championship to Anfield, and possibly the F A Cup as well. Interviewed by the *Liverpool Echo*, Shankly declared, 'I feel much better now than before the previous two seasons. In one, we started off in the Second Division; in the other we were newly promoted to the First Division. I had some apprehension then; now it has gone. I think we are equal to or better than any other team. If we think along these lines we shall be.'

He went on to talk about the training methods at Melwood and claimed that the famous 'sweat box', which was a set of boards placed fifteen yards

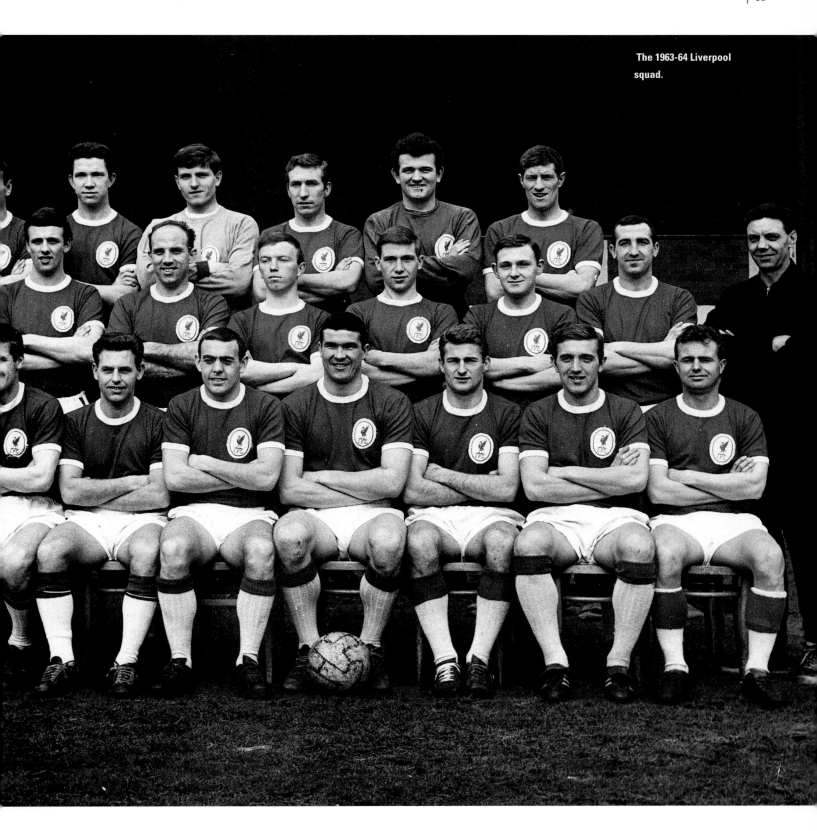

The 1963-64 Liverpool squad.

apart, which a player would go into and then have to blast the ball from board to board for as long as possible, would give the Liverpool team an edge in fitness over most teams in the League. 'My pet theme is that we shall never get anywhere if we don't work. All our training functions are well thought out. If players think they can add anything to them we will listen.'

Asking his players to contribute their opinions on aspects of training and match-play would be a feature of Shankly's tactics during the coming season.

* * *

Liverpool actually started their Championship season in disastrous fashion. Although they picked up points away from home, at Anfield they lost their first three games on the trot. Legend has it that Shankly strode into the boardroom after the third

Everton and Liverpool in 1964 before a derby game; Everton won 3-1.

that they were over anxious to do well in front of their home supporters. When the heart-to-heart drew to a close, Shankly knew that he had to work fast to prepare his team for that evening's game against Wolves. They had beaten the Midlands club 3-1 at Molineux the previous week, but that was away from the white-hot atmosphere of Anfield. Shankly got to work on sending his team out in a more relaxed frame of mind to try to obtain their first home win of the season.

The pep talk did the trick and they thrashed Wolves 6-0. But Liverpool's inconsistent start to the new campaign continued the following Saturday when they lost 3-0 away to Sheffield United. The following Saturday, however, Anfield was to witness the victory they had craved for since the 1950s, the defeat of arch rivals, and reigning champions, Everton. Close on 52,000 saw two goals from Ian Callaghan, with a late reply from Roy Vernon, win the day for Liverpool.

Local hero Callaghan, overjoyed to be the match winner, after the game described his opening goal as a 25-yard 'Bobby Charlton special' that flew past West in the Everton goal. 'As I got the ball, the defence suddenly fell away from me and to my surprise, gave me a clear sight of goal. I thought, this is too good to last and so I shot.'

No greater compliment could be paid to the ferocity of Callaghan's piledriver than the *Liverpool Echo*'s correspondent who wrote, 'The shot was as hard as anything Billy Liddell ever delivered. If he plays at Anfield for 50 seasons, Callaghan will never hit one with such power and such lethal direction.'

* * *

The derby victory kick-started Liverpool's season in dramatic style and they went on to win eight of their next nine games. Probably the most crucial of all these victories as Liverpool powered their way to the top of the table was their 1-0 victory against Manchester United at Old Trafford. Ron Yeats scored the goal that won the game, his first for the club; he was beginning to display a quality of play that was more than just that of a stopper centre-half. Roger Hunt was also now blossoming into a

defeat and said to the directors, 'I can assure you, gentlemen, that we will win a game at Anfield this season!' and then left the room.

On the Monday morning, Shankly told all his first-team players to attend a meeting after training. During the post-mortem, he asked every one of his players for their suggestions on why they were failing to show the form they were capable of at Anfield. The general consensus amongst them was

'We love you, Yeah, Yeah, Yeah'; the victory celebration at Anfield after Liverpool's title success.

formidable goal scorer and in one game against Stoke, blasted in four goals in 34 minutes of goal-scoring at its finest. It was during this Christmas fixture against Stoke, which Liverpool went on to win 6-1, that the Kop took to singing Beatles' songs to display their pride; not only just in their heroes in red shirts on the pitch, but also the pride they felt in watching their fellow Scousers, John, Paul, George and Ringo take the pop world by storm. As thousands of Koppites sang 'We love you, Yeah! Yeah! Yeah!' over and over again, Boxing Day at Anfield in 1963 was a fabulous place to be.

A few weeks later, Anfield was treated to another goals bonanza as Liverpool thrashed Sheffield United 6-1, Kop idol Ian St John grabbing a hat-trick. It was Willie Stevenson, however, who the *Liverpool Echo* voted their man of the match: 'He varies his production of the ball, he can angle a short telling pass or punch one down the centre with the artistry one only associates with wing halves of top class.'

It was during the Easter period that Liverpool really emerged as Championship contenders. On Good Friday, Hunt scored a hat-trick against Spurs at White Hart Lane to give them a 3-1 victory. The following day, Liverpool travelled to Leicester to take on their bogey team. Another 3-1 win put Liverpool in great heart for their Easter Monday clash with Spurs back at Anfield. Two goals from St John and one from Alf Arrowsmith, who was proving himself somewhat of a sensation after the injury to midfield general Jimmy Melia prompted Shankly to move St John into a deeper role with Arrowsmith and Roger Hunt up front, gave Liverpool a comfortable victory. Bill Shankly was later to claim that playing St John in midfield and introducing Arrowsmith into the team were important factors in Liverpool's Championship victory.

Liverpool's next game was against their Championship rivals Manchester United, and Alf Arrowsmith, once again displayed his considerable promise, scoring two, with Callaghan adding another as Liverpool ran out comfortable 3-0 winners. It appeared that even the combined talents of Charlton, Law and Best couldn't stop the

TOMMY LAWRENCE

Tommy Lawrence signed as a professional for Liverpool in 1957, but had to wait until 1962 to make his League debut. Injury to Jim Furnell saw Lawrence thrust into the team to play at West Brom. Liverpool lost 1–0, but Lawrence kept his place until the end of the season.

It was during Liverpool's Championship season of 1963-64 that Lawrence established himself not just as a First Division goalkeeper, but also winning international recognition by Scotland as well.

There is a tendency to sometimes forget just what a vital role Lawrence played in Liverpool's great success of the 1960s, but the fact that he missed only a handful of games in a six-season period shows just what a consistent performer between the sticks he was. During one season, 1968-69, he conceded just 24 goals in the First Division. In the season of 1970-71, Tommy Lawrence lost his place to the emerging future goal-keeping great, Ray Clemence, but the part that he played in Shankly's first great team will never be forgotten by the Anfield faithful of this period.

Lawrence ended his career across the Mersey at Tranmere Rovers.

Tommy Lawrence holding the base of the F A Cup as Liverpool celebrate their victory in 1965

Red Machine from powering their way to the title.

Liverpool clinched the First Division Championship, fittingly at Anfield against Arsenal. This time it was wing maestro Peter Thompson who scored a brace, with further goals from St John, Arrowsmith and Hunt allowing Liverpool to demolish the London team 5-0. Shankly's prophecy that the title would come to Anfield had come true.

* * *

The acclamation that the new champions received was even more euphoric than the reception Liverpool were given when they won promotion two years earlier. The Kop serenaded the crestfallen Arsenal team as they waited for the final whistle to end their misery with a rendition of 'London Bridge Is Falling Down'. After they had departed the scene, the Kop choir went into full swing, hailing their heroes with chant after chant of 'Liverpool, Liverpool'. The team paraded around Anfield with a home-made replica of the championship trophy

IAN CALLAGHAN

'He is a truly great professional who has never caused anybody a scrap of trouble. Ian Callaghan is everything good that a man can be. No praise is too high for him!' When Bill Shankly penned this tribute to 'Cally' in the Liverpool players' autobiography in 1975, the Liverpool midfielder had several seasons playing at the top still to come.

Callaghan's final tally of 843 appearances for the club will probably never be surpassed. He was the only player who was a first-team performer in the Second Division and was still a regular when Shankly retired in 1974.

'When Ian came here as a young boy, he weighed no more than 8 stone. We had to go easy on him in training. If we'd hammered him, he mightn't have become the player who has broken the record number of League appearances,' was Shankly's memory of the Liverpool-born youngster that he brought to the first team at the end of season 1959-60.

Several years later, Callaghan established himself in the first team and formed an outstanding wing partnership with Peter Thompson. Both were instrumental in Liverpool's outstanding success of the mid 1960s, and although always known for his gentlemanly conduct, Tommy Smith once remarked of Callaghan, 'Ian was never a dirty player, but you would think twice about getting stuck into him. He was so small and compact, he only got booked once in his whole career but I can assure you that Cally was just as lethal as myself.'

Callaghan's career took a new direction in the early 1970s when Shankly switched him from the wing into midfield, and he took to his new role so well that in 1977, at the age of thirty-five, he was capped twice more by England, his two other international caps being won during the mid-1960s. Though never a player to grab the headlines, Callaghan was crucial in Liverpool's emergence as one of the greatest club sides.

Bob Paisley summed up Callaghan, 'Sometimes you'll be told that a player needs to have a nasty streak to get on in the game. Ian is one lad who showed that you could be as nice as pie and still make it at the top level.'

that a fan had handed to captain Ron Yeats; the real thing still taking pride of place in the trophy room across Stanley Park at Everton. Rumours were that Everton had refused to hand over the trophy.

One local reporter despatched to Anfield to cover the game, admitted that he was even more captivated by the occasion as a whole: 'I've never seen anything to match this in all the years I've been attending. It was the Anfield crowd's day. There have been occasions in the past when one has been almost ashamed to say one came from "Liverpule". This behaviour at a match which had everything at stake made one proud to be remotely associated with a city finding fame afresh for its standards of football and now for crowd behaviour. From an hour before kick-off until nearly three hours later, this was a Liverpool crowd at its Sunday best.'

The fact that the BBC not only sent camera crews to cover the game, but also for a feature on the Kop to be shown in Monday evening's *Panorama* current affairs programme gives one an idea of the national interest that was being shown in the phenomenon that the Anfield supporters had now become.

* * *

Football fans had sung before at games, but not with the passion, humour and spontaneity of the Kop. Social anthropologists pondered over who organised it all – did they practice in the pub before the game? Did someone hand out sheets with chants and songs printed on them? The answer was that it was all spontaneous. It began with chants in homage to their favourite players and after the advent of the Beatles and other Merseybeat bands such as Gerry and the Pacemakers, they decided to change the words slightly, thus 'She Loves You'

The Liverpool League-Championship-winning team, 1964.

With the Beatles taking the US by storm, the full Liverpool tour party were invited to be guests on **The Ed Sullivan Show**. Bill Shankly didn't enjoy this 1964 US tour and declined the offer to appear on the programme.

became 'We Love You'. Other Kop favourites of the time such as 'Ee-Aye-Addio' could be traced back to songs and chants sung by Liverpool children in street games. When watching fans at other clubs witnessed the singing and chanting of the Kop on *Match of the Day* it was inevitable that they would imitate this at their own grounds. Few, however, were ever able to match the sheer inventiveness of the Liverpool fans of the 1960s. It was a phenomenon that will probably never be witnessed again, not even at Anfield.

* * *

With the championship safely won, Shankly, who normally drilled into his players that every game had to be treated like a Cup final, with maximum effort for the full 90 minutes, relaxed a little and displayed a more facetious side to his character. He took goalkeeper Tommy Lawrence to one side during training and told him, 'Tom, wouldn't it be great if we could put a deck chair in the middle of the goal, you sitting in it, cigar in your mouth, and when the ball comes, you get out of your deck chair and catch it and say, "It's a lovely day to play football, isn't it?"'

Tommy decided not to put into practice his boss's idea, but Liverpool did ease up a little, losing two of their final three games.

THE FIRST DIVISION
18 April 1964

Liverpool	**5**
Arsenal	**0**

Liverpool made sure of the First Division title with this emphatic victory over Arsenal. Their five-goal winning margin meant that they had scored 21 goals in their last seven games, with only two against. It was this run of seven victories that swept them to the title. St John opened the scoring, but Arsenal were given the opportunity to draw level when Yeats handled in the penalty area. George Eastham hit a hard penalty kick to Lawrence's left, but the Liverpool goalkeeper pulled off a stunning save. Liverpool made Arsenal pay for this when Arrowsmith headed home to make it 2-0.

After the interval, Liverpool put on an exhibition of football that left the Londoners dazzled. Peter Thompson in particular was unstoppable, and it was Thompson who scored Liverpool's third in the 53rd minute. He beat his marker, not once, but twice, and then unleashed a thunderous shot that goalkeeper Furnell could only palm into the net. Just five minutes later, it was Thompson again who showed the ball to Arsenal full-back Magill before sprinting past him and blasting the ball past Furnell. 'London Bridge is falling down' chanted the Anfield crowd, and just minutes later, it collapsed completely when Roger Hunt hammered home Liverpool's fifth. 'Ee-aye-addio, we won the League' was now the cry ringing around the ground. The title was back at Anfield for the sixth time in Liverpool's history. Liverpool's attack was still hungry for more goals and only a handling offence on the line stopped Arrowsmith scoring a sixth. The Kop chanted for Liverpool goalkeeper Tommy Lawrence to step up and take the penalty. Lawrence's team-mates also tried to coax him to join in the goal feast. But Tommy was reluctant and it was left to Callaghan to take the kick. The beleaguered Arsenal goalkeeper Furnell pulled off a fine save to deny the Liverpool winger, and the day's scoring was brought to an end.

The Kop forgave Tommy Lawrence for not complying with their wishes immediately when they sang 'We have the finest goalkeeper in the land' in honour of their hero.

At the end of the game, incredible scenes followed, with Liverpool captain Ron Yeats parading a home-made replica of the Championship trophy around a jubilant Anfield. The supporters chanted for the players and then Bill Shankly. Shankly gave a wave of acknowledgement to the fans, who roared their appreciation. Arsenal manager Billy Wright was quick to pay tribute to Liverpool after the game when he said, 'Liverpool are really worthy champions, make no mistake about it'.

At the post-match celebrations, Liverpool directors and players heaped praise upon their guiding light, manager Bill Shankly. 'He's the greatest in the world' was the general comment. But Shankly would have none of it, saying, 'We are a working-class team. We've no room for fancy footballers. Just workers who will respond to the demands I lay down. Liverpool's triumph is no one-man affair. My training and coaching staff have done a wonderful job. Every man in our organisation has been taught the importance of looking after the small things, for it's surprising how they can add up to really important things. From the boardroom to the groundsman, every cog in the machine has functioned perfectly. Everyone has given 100 per cent effort.'

Liverpool: Lawrence, Byrne, Moran, Milne, Yeats, Stevenson, Callaghan, Hunt, St John, Arrowsmith, Thompson

Arsenal: Furnell, Magill, McCullough, Neill, Ure, Sneddon, Skirton, Strong, Baker, Eastham, Armstrong

*We are a working-class team. We've
no room for fancy footballers. Just
workers who will respond to the
demands I lay down.'*
Bill Shankly

Roger Hunt in action
against Arsenal in
Liverpool's 5-0 victory
that clinched the 1964
Championship.

CHAPTER FIVE

1964-65

THE F A CUP AT LAST!
Shankly's Red Army
At Wembley

*Gerry looked at me and pleaded, "Don't
tell anyone." I asked, "Do you know your
collarbone is broken?" Gerry nodded.
He insisted on playing on through the
remaining 82 minutes and extra time.
It was one of the bravest Wembley
displays I ever witnessed.
Leeds never knew – they thought it
was his shin that was injured.'*
Bob Paisley, on Gerry Byrnes's 1965 Cup final display

When **Liverpool reported back** for pre-
season training at the beginning of the
1964-65 season, Shankly and his squad were
greeted with shock news. Key player, Ian St John,
was recovering in a local hospital after a rushed
appendix operation. The cause of the problem was
the stone from a date that Ian had eaten during the
Christmas period. Ian showed his visitors the full-
sized stone, which he had been given by the
medical staff as a memento of his operation.
Although Shankly was renowned for ignoring
injuries to his players, unless they were chronic, this
was one occasion when he had to accept that one
of the vital cogs in his Liverpool team wouldn't be
available until well into the season. Nevertheless,
Shankly and his players were in high spirits. They

Gerry Byrne and Gordon Milne parade the F A Cup at Anfield before the 1965 Inter Milan game.

had their first-ever adventures into Europe to look forward to and they were confident that they could build on the success of the previous campaign. They also had a new chairman, Sidney Reakes, who had taken over from T. V. Williams, who was now club president.

Williams had decided to make way for a younger man but was keen to point out that he would still do all he could to assist the club and players. Speaking to his local paper, he suggested that the success of Liverpool would soon result in bigger pay packets for the team, 'If they put up good performances, they will get good gates, and if they get good gates, they will get something for the kitty and their days of retirement.'

But within a year, there would be upheaval over financial rewards at Anfield. Bill Shankly, never one to dwell over money matters, concerned himself only with the coming season. He told his team, 'I said this time last year that a fit Liverpool who fought hard were capable of beating anyone. This you bore out by lifting the championship of England, which is really the championship of Great Britain. We have simple training methods and a simple, but positive way of playing. If you carry it out with the same dedication, you'll win the title again.'

He then went on to talk to the press who were curious about Liverpool's training methods. 'It's simple,' claimed the Liverpool boss. 'The system is based on exhaustion and recovery, building up players' stamina to enable them to produce their inherent skill and footballing ability, despite the speed of the game, from the first minute to the 90th.'

Although the press accepted Shankly's explanation of his training formula, there was still the nagging feeling that the Liverpool boss was holding back on a secret training formula that gave his team the edge over most others. Within football, the secrets of Liverpool's success would grow into mythical proportions with the coming years, but Shankly was revealing all; the Liverpool secret of success was based predominantly on simplicity and hard work.

As with everything that took place at Anfield, Shankly's preparation for the coming campaign left nothing to chance. The players' level of fitness would gradually be built up, with the risk of strains and pulled muscles kept to a minimum. Practice games would begin initially on a full-size pitch, before progressing to just half the playing area. Eventually, with a higher level of fitness now achieved, the players would play five-a-side in a quarter of the pitch to allow them to sharpen up their first touch and distribution; the confined area of play allowing no time to dwell on the ball.

* * *

Liverpool's opening game of the season was actually the away tie in the opening round of the European Cup. They were due to play Icelandic champions Reykjavik and Shankly was determined that their first European adventure would be something to remember.

Ron Yeats still chuckles when he recalls their trip to Iceland. 'It was unbelievable, we travelled from Liverpool to Manchester, Manchester to London and then Shanks decided that when we touched down at Prestwick, he would show us around Ayrshire, where he came from, before the final flight to Iceland. He then had a coach waiting for us in Scotland to take us to Butlins Holiday Camp. We all trooped on to the coach and when we arrived at Butlins, Shanks introduced himself to the fellow on the door: "Bill Shankly, manager of Liverpool Football Club *en route* to Iceland to play in the European Cup." The man on the door shook his head and said, "I think you've taken the wrong road Sir!" I can't say what Shanks said to the fellow, but we were all marched back on to the coach. We were bursting to laugh, but daren't.'

Liverpool won the tie easily 11-1 over the two legs, and were drawn to meet the formidable Belgian champions Anderlecht in the next round.

* * *

Liverpool's only new signing to strengthen the squad for the coming season was the Manchester United forward Phil Chisnall, with Arsenal's Geoff Strong joining later in the season. Liverpool's opening League game of the season was against the

Shankly inspects the Anfield pitch with match officials before the European Cup tie against Cologne in 1965.

team they had thrashed just a few months earlier to clinch the tie, Arsenal. This time the Londoners made Liverpool fight all the way for a 3-2 victory, two of the Liverpool goals coming from Gordon Wallace who was deputising for the recuperating Ian St John. This game was also chosen by the BBC for their inaugural *Match of the Day* programme.

As with the previous season, however, Liverpool didn't start the new campaign too convincingly. The absence of St John hit the team severely, and Liverpool were also unfortunate to be without Alf Arrowsmith, who had sustained a bad knee injury in a Charity Shield game against West Ham.

Liverpool lost five of their first eight games and it looked as though retaining the Championship was slipping out of their reach. Shankly introduced nineteen-year-old Bobby Graham into the team for the home game against Aston Villa, and the young Scot was an immediate sensation, scoring a hat-trick in Liverpool's 5-1 victory. Graham scored again when Liverpool defeated Sheffield United 3-1 in their next game, but in general, their League form during the 1964-65 season was disappointing and inconsistent.

The signing of Geoff Strong, whom Shankly converted into one of the most efficient utility players in England, and the emergence of Liverpool teenager Tommy Smith added much-needed depth to the squad, but it was to be only in the Cup competitions that Liverpool would shine this season. Tommy Smith had actually made his Liverpool debut at home to Birmingham in May 1963, but had to wait until August of 1964 for his next first-team League outing. Shankly recalled that Smith grew so impatient waiting for another chance that he decided to take matters into his own hands. Shankly said, 'He was always knocking on the door to ask when he was going to get a first-team chance. One day we were playing five-a-side and Tommy slid into Chris Lawler and caught him on the ankle. Chris's ankle went up like a balloon. We were all disturbed about Chris. As we were coming off the training ground, Tommy said to me, "Will I be in the team on Saturday?" He'd just crippled Chris and then

The new all-red strip –
Liverpool revealed their
new kit in their European
Cup tie against
Anderlecht in November
1964.

wanted to know would he be in the team; he was.'

Once he was established in the Liverpool team, Tommy Smith became a permanent and vital cog in the Shankly team that would achieve so much success over the next two seasons. Although renowned for his hard tackling, Smith had much more to his game that that. 'You don't play over 600 times for Liverpool under great managers like Shankly and Paisley, if all you can do is kick people,' he once angrily proclaimed; and he was right.

* * *

Although struggling in the League, Liverpool were enjoying their first venture into Europe. Belgian champions, Anderlecht would provide far stiffer

opposition than Liverpool's first-round victims Reykjavik, but the Shankly team managed to come through the tie without too much difficulty. It was prior to the home-leg that Shankly, always on the look-out for a psychological advantage over his opponents, decided to change the Liverpool strip to all red for the first time. He told Ron Yeats to put on the new strip and run out of the tunnel. Shankly stood on the pitch and couldn't hide his glee: 'Jesus Christ, son, you look bloody massive. You'll scare them to death!'

The all-red strip that became Liverpool's trade-mark, was here to stay. 'It'll make the team look even tougher, bigger and more formidable to the

TOMMY SMITH

'You don't play over 600 games for Liverpool, under great managers like Bill Shankly and Bob Paisley if all you can do is kick people,' is Tommy Smith's response to anyone who dares to imply that all he ever was was a hatchet man.

Born within walking distance of Anfield, Smith joined the club straight from school and signed professional forms on his seventeenth birthday. Smith freely admits that he was encouraged to foster his 'hardman' image by Bill Shankly during his early days at the club: 'I used to get stuck in and was afraid of nobody. I was taught as a fifteen-year-old by Shanks that who could I have to fear. Shanks used to say, "Just hand them a hospital menu, son!" It's quite laughable when you think about it, but sometimes, it worked If you can break somebody's concentration from the word go, you have immediately got an advantage. Down the years, I have uttered my little warnings to some of the game's greats. Shanks and Bob Paisley used to say, "Rattle his bones when you go into a tackle."'

By the mid 1960s, Tommy Smith had established himself in the Liverpool team. He was as adept at playing in midfield as defence, and in the 1970s won more honours playing at right-back.

Bob Paisley summed up Tommy Smith perfectly when he remarked, 'Tommy is as honest as the day is long. If you wanted someone who gave you absolutely everything each time he pulled on a Liverpool jersey, you couldn't look beyond him.'

Tommy Smith (left) with Tommy Lawrence

opposition,' Shankly told the press and when one thinks about it, it actually did.

After giving his team a pre-match pep talk, the gist of it being that the Belgian team were rubbish and should feel privileged to be on the same pitch as the Champions of England, Liverpool crushed Anderlecht quite comfortably 3-0. After the game, an animated Shankly told his team, 'Christ, boys, you've just beaten one of the finest teams in Europe!'

The return leg in Belgium was due to take place just before the Christmas holiday period on 16 December but the journey wasn't without incident. The Viscount airliner that was due to fly the team to Belgium was at the centre of an emergency alert at Liverpool airport. As Shankly and his team waited in the terminal building for the aircraft to arrive, the captain of the Viscount contacted air traffic control to relay the news to them that smoke was entering the flight deck. Emergency services and fire engines stood by as the stricken plane touched down at Liverpool. Thankfully, the aircraft was

CHRIS LAWLER

Chris Lawler was another product of Liverpool schools' football. He made his debut in 1962 and by season 1964-65 was in possession of the right-back spot in the team. He was an England schoolboy international and went on to play for the full England team on four occasions.

Always capable of popping-up with important goals, Lawler scored 61 times for Liverpool, a remarkable figure for a full-back. He was dubbed 'the Silent Knight' by the Kop – a reference to his modest and quiet demeanour, both on and off the pitch. 'Sometimes you would see Tommy Smith, his great pal, bawling at him during a game. Smithy never wrapped anything up. And if you looked closely enough, you might see Chris answering back – but out of the side of his mouth. Chris never shouted the odds, but in his own quiet way, he was as hard a character as the rest,' recalled Bob Paisley.

Lawler made over 500 appearances for Liverpool before signing for Portsmouth in 1975. His contribution to the outstanding Liverpool teams of the 1960s and early 1970s is immeasurable.

brought safely to ground and the fire was traced to a short-circuit in the electric system. Eventually, the twenty-four-strong Liverpool party set off safely on their way to Belgium, but it was incidents such as that that led to Shankly always being the most reluctant of travellers.

A Roger Hunt goal gave Liverpool a 1-0 victory in front of 60,000 frustrated Anderlecht supporters. The rest of Europe was beginning to take notice of an emerging red threat from Liverpool.

* * *

Liverpool's League form had also now become more consistent and they remained unbeaten from November 1964 through to 27 February 1965. Victories over West Brom and Stockport in the Cup also pleased Shankly, who knew that the prize that every Liverpudlian wanted above all others was the FA Cup.

The draw for the next round of the European Cup paired Liverpool with German club F C Cologne. The first leg took place in Cologne and it turned out to be quite a trip for Liverpool, with the Mayor of Liverpool and a delegation of civic dignitaries travelling to Germany to support the Reds, using the occasion to cement the long-standing friendship between the two cities. Lord

The Cologne goalkeeper challenges Ian St John for the ball during their 1965 European Cup tie.

Mayor, Alderman Louis Caplan, said, 'I met the burgomaster last summer and I know he is a keen supporter of Cologne, so I hope to prepare the way for a civic delegation from Cologne to come back to Liverpool for the return match.' The Liverpool players returned home, quietly satisfied with themselves after a hard-fought 0-0 draw. The return leg at Anfield, however, proved equally as tough and once again, there was no score. A third game was arranged at a neutral venue, which turned out to be Rotterdam, and once again, the match finished all square at 2-2. The outcome now had to be decided on the toss of a coin. It was a nerve-racking moment for Shankly and his team as captain Ron

Yeats stepped up with the Cologne captain to decide who would go through to the European Cup semi-finals. Ron Yeats recalled, 'When it came to the toss of the coin, I thought "get in quick". I said, "I'll have tails, referee," and the referee said, "Okay, Liverpool tails, Cologne heads." When he tossed it, I couldn't believe it. It stuck in a divot on its side. The referee picked up the coin and tossed it again. It came down tails. I could see Shanks at the side of the pitch. He said to me as I walked off, "Well done, big man, what did you pick?" I said tails. "I would have picked that myself," said Shanks and he just walked away. I was waiting for the adulation but he just walked away.'

THE F A CUP SEMI-FINAL
27 March 1965

| Liverpool | 2 |
| Chelsea | 0 |

With Chelsea riding high at the top of the First Division, and Liverpool expected to be jaded from a gruelling European Cup tie against Cologne just days earlier, the Londoners went into the game as slight favourites.

Bill Shankly had always maintained that the training methods he employed gave his team a fitness and power of recuperation which allowed them an edge over their opponents, and once again, he was proved correct. Liverpool totally outplayed and outstayed Tommy Docherty's talented Chelsea team, Liverpool dominating the game from the start, with Milne, Stevenson and St John holding complete midfield domination over their Chelsea counterparts of Hollins, Harris and Venables.

After a goalless first half, the only surprise being how Liverpool had failed to take the lead, the expected resurgence of Chelsea after the break failed to materialise. It was inevitable that a Liverpool goal would come, and when it did, it was a Peter Thompson special. St John hit a 30-yard pass to the winger, who controlled the ball instantly and then sped past Hinton and Hollins. He now had only Bonetti in the Chelsea goal to beat and after taking aim, drove the ball past the goalkeeper before he had a chance to cover the shot.

Chelsea attempted to hit back, but the Liverpool defence, with Smith, playing alongside Yeats, having an outstanding game for a youth of twenty, kept a firm grip on Tambling, Bridges and Graham. Liverpool clinched the game 12 minutes from time after Ron Harris brought down St John in the penalty area. St John, who had had an outstanding game, had clashed with Harris several times during the match, and on one occasion, a late tackle by the Chelsea hardman resulted in St John retaliating by punching Harris to the ground. The tenacious Scot was booked for this misdemeanour. Gordon Milne was Liverpool's recognised penalty taker, but on this occasion Willie Stevenson stepped up to take it. He said after the game, 'I wasn't due to take any penalties for us. Gordon Milne should have taken the kick, but when St John was brought down, I immediately said to Milne, "I'll take it". It was the first I have taken for Liverpool and I think I'll retire as undefeated penalty taker.' Stevenson made no mistake with the kick and Liverpool were now certain of their place at Wembley.

Late in the game, Terry Venables also had his name taken for a foul on St John, but by now, Chelsea were a spent force. 20,000 travelling Liverpool fans danced a jig of happiness at the final whistle. Peter Thompson was carried shoulder-high off the pitch by the cheering fans and later remarked, 'I was a member of the Preston team that put Liverpool out of the Cup a few years ago. I hope I have repaid the debt by helping to send Liverpool to Wembley.'

Chelsea manager, Tommy Docherty, was obviously bitterly disappointed that his young team hadn't done themselves justice in what was in many ways a one-sided semi-final. But he gave credit to the reds: 'Liverpool were far the better side. All our boys were fit and fresh, and Liverpool had a hard game in mid-week. Bill Shankly must be a very proud man. I would be under similar circumstances.'

The Liverpool manager was indeed thrilled, telling the press, 'The team did the talking for me on the field. It was a tremendous performance considering the punishing game we had against Cologne in Rotterdam on Wednesday night. I thought we showed more class in the key positions.' Liverpool's trainer, Bob Paisley, who had missed out on an F A Cup final place so cruelly after scoring the semi-final winner, fifteen years earlier, said with a twinkle in his eye, 'That little warm-up against Cologne on Wednesday did us good!'

Liverpool: Lawrence, Lawler, Byrne, Milne, Yeats, Stevenson, Callaghan, Hunt, St John, Smith, Thompson

Chelsea: Bonetti, Hinton, McCreadie, Hollins, Mortimore, Harris, Murray, Graham, Bridges, Venables, Tambling

advantage of an exhausted Liverpool team. Bill Shankly had always proclaimed to anyone who would listen that his team were by far the fittest group of players in Britain and in the semi-final Liverpool proved this was no idle boast. Chelsea did match Liverpool until just after the hour mark, but then Peter Thompson struck and Wembley was within their sights. Willie Stevenson added another from the penalty spot and the game was won. Shankly's life-long friend, Tommy Docherty, admitted that Chelsea were beaten by a superior team on the day.

Liverpool's opponents at Wembley were to be Don Revie's Leeds United; a team that were as hard, as fit, but, for the time being, not yet as talented as Shankly's Liverpool. Winning the F A Cup for the first time in their history wouldn't be easy for Ron Yeats and company.

Once Liverpool had booked their Wembley place, Merseyside went into a football frenzy; particularly when it came to the pursuit of the ever elusive Cup final ticket. Liverpool fans' expectations were high that they would deliver the Cup back to Anfield, and they all wanted to be at Wembley to witness the historic event. Liverpool's average gate at Anfield during the 1964-65 season was over 41,000, but Liverpool's Wembley allocation was only 15,000 tickets. Liverpool were inundated with phone calls and begging letters from fans desperate for tickets. Bill Shankly attempted to obtain as many tickets as he could to supply the fans who supported the team week in and week out. 'Any tickets I've got are going to the boys on the Kop,' he angrily told one caller from Birmingham who claimed that he'd been a Liverpool fan all his life. Liverpool Chairman Sidney Reakes received a phone call from Leeds United Supporters Club, requesting a ticket, as a gesture of goodwill between the clubs, for the newly crowned beauty queen Miss Leeds United. Apparently Leeds had turned down this request themselves, so the Supporters Club decided to try Liverpool.

* * *

With the Cup final approaching Liverpool did ease off in the League, using the remaining weeks of the

Peter Thompson (with ball), scorer of a brilliant goal against Chelsea in the F A Cup semi-final in 1965.

With a place in the European Cup semi-finals now in the bag, Liverpool turned their attention back to domestic matters. Just three days after their energy-sapping exploits in the European Cup, Liverpool were due to meet Chelsea in the F A Cup semi-final at Villa Park. Liverpool had disposed of bogey team, Leicester City, in the quarter-finals after a replay and were now confident that this would finally be the year that the F A Cup would come to Anfield.

Tommy Docherty's Chelsea were only too pleased to watch Liverpool struggle to overcome Cologne on television just a few days prior to the semi, and were confident that they would take season to rest some of the first-teamers and allow others time to recover from injuries. The unlucky Gordon Milne was trying desperately to get himself fit for the final, but was destined not to recover in time. Interviewed a few days before the final, Bill Shankly told the Liverpool Echo that he had personally watched Leeds three times during the past two weeks and considered that they were at their most dangerous at set pieces. When the questioning turned to tickets, Shankly told the *Echo*, 'Correspondence has become mountainous since we reached the final. There are pleas for tickets in every post from people I haven't seen or heard of for years. It's simply impossible to help them.'

When the day of the final arrived, Shankly had his team well prepared. Unfortunately, Gordon Milne's knee injury kept him out, but the other doubt, Ian Callaghan was declared fit to play,

although only after continuous treatment. During the train journey to London, in fact, Bob Paisley sat with Callaghan in the guards van continually applying iced-water compresses to the Liverpool winger's leg until the train arrived in the capital. Paisley's dedicated treatment did the trick and Callaghan, with his perpetual running, was a key factor in Liverpool's success. After missing out in the League to Manchester United on goal average, Leeds were just as desperate to win the Cup as Liverpool. A classic battle of the roses was anticipated, but, as so often happens in Cup finals, the tension of the occasion affected both teams, and neither played to their full potential. Liverpool's hopes took a blow early in the game when full-bank Gerry Byrne was on the receiving end of a crunching challenge from the diminutive but hard-as-iron Leeds captain Bobby Collins. Byrne

Don Revie and Bill Shankly, two great managers of the 1960s and 1970s, lead out their teams before the 1965 F A Cup final.

Willie Stevenson shoots marginally wide in the F A Cup final against Leeds in 1965.

sustained a broken collar bone in the collision, but managed to keep the extent of his injury from the Leeds camp, and even Shankly himself refused to believe Bob Paisley when he told the Liverpool boss that the full-back's collar bone was fractured. Byrne was obviously in extreme pain but the heroic full-back played out not only the whole game, but extra time as well. Substitutes hadn't yet been introduced into the British game, so for a ten-man Liverpool to have beaten a formidable Leeds team would have been highly unlikely.

After a dour 90 minutes, the game ended in stalemate. The deadlock was finally broken when three minutes into extra-time, when Byrne sent in a cross for Roger Hunt to open the scoring. The Liverpool contingent at Wembley went berserk. 'Ee-aye-addio, we've won the Cup' rang around the stadium. Just eight minutes later their singing came to a sudden halt as Billy Bremner, a player who never stopped trying until the game was over, struck an equaliser for Leeds. Liverpool were stunned. With just nine minutes remaining of the second period of extra-time, Liverpool's Mr Perpetual Motion, Ian Callaghan, fired in a cross for Ian St John to fling himself forward and bullet the ball past Gary Sprake. A crestfallen Leeds didn't recover from this blow and the F A Cup was Liverpool's.

Wembley had never witnessed celebrations like it, as Ron Yeats stepped up to take the trophy. It was a mixture of euphoria and relief that the Liverpudlians felt as they stood and cheered their team as they paraded around Wembley. No longer would Evertonians be able to sneer at them as they posed the question 'When are Liverpool going to win the Cup?' The Cup was now theirs; Shankly, their messiah, had delivered the goods yet again. As the rest of the nation watched on television as the joyous scenes unfolded, they now knew that the men from Anfield had fully arrived as a soccer force.

* * *

In later years, Shankly spoke of the satisfaction that winning the Cup brought him. 'I thought it was a terrible disgrace that Liverpool had had to suffer the taunts for 73 years that they hadn't won the F A Cup. Never mind winning the European Cup; winning the F A Cup was the hardest thing.' The reception that greeted the triumphant Liverpool team when they arrived back in the city for their homecoming hadn't been witnessed since the days of Dixie Dean and his Everton team parading around Liverpool with the Cup in 1933.

Bill Shankly's wife, Nessie, who very rarely attended football matches, was at Wembley in 1965 and still has vivid memories of the homecoming. 'We arrived at Lime Street station and I'd never seen such crowds. They were ecstatic. That really was our first experience of the Liverpool people proper. Bill was over the moon, as we all were.' It was estimated that over 250,000 lined the city centre streets as the Liverpool coach drove towards the Town Hall. To Shankly, the real joy of winning was in sharing his, and his team's, happiness with the multitudes who supported them, and in witnessing the joy Liverpool's victory had brought to the people of the city. It was almost as if he was more pleased for them than for himself.

Roger Hunt, reflecting on Liverpool's F A Cup victory in 1965, recently commented, 'The fantastic enthusiasm of those fans underlined to me that playing a part in bringing the Cup back to Anfield ranked as my greatest achievement at the time. Even in the light of what happened afterwards [England's World Cup victory in 1966], I'm not sure that I ever topped it.'

* * *

Watching Liverpool's Wembley victory with interest at their Southport headquarters were Inter Milan

manager Helenio Herrera and his team. Just three days after their Cup victory, Liverpool were due to meet Inter in the first leg of the European Cup semi-final. Herrera was suitably impressed and told the press that he expected a very hard match. The Inter manager was probably quietly confident that his team would be able to contain the new English Cup holders without too much difficulty. He knew all about the energy-sapping Wembley turf, and with extra-time being played as well, Liverpool were bound to be a little leg weary. The Liverpool that he saw against Leeds was also not Shankly's team at their best. On the evening of the game, Anfield was packed nearly two hours before kick-off time.

Ron Yeats remembered arriving at an almost eerie ground with few people in the outlying streets. 'We didn't realize everyone was inside the ground. When our team bus arrived there was nobody outside the ground. The police had actually requested that Liverpool open the turnstiles at 3.30 to ease the congestion in the streets and by 5.30, the gates of the Kop were closed.'

Shankly, as ever relentless in his pursuit of a psychological advantage over the opposition, decided to send Wembley hero Gerry Byrne and Liverpool's other injured star, Gordon Milne, out early to parade the F A Cup in front of the fans. Shankly's ploy did the trick and the duo received a tremendous reception. Apparently, the Kop had been singing prior to this gesture 'Ee-aye-addio, we wanna see the Cup'. Shankly heard this and decided to comply with the Kop's wishes. The Inter team were actually out on the pitch warming up when Byrne and Milne emerged with it. Although the Italians were experienced European campaigners, the roar of the Kop must have unsettled them. Shankly didn't really need to give his team a pep talk.

Tommy Smith says that Shankly said very little. 'Shanks never put any fear into us. He just said get out there and enjoy it. We'd won the F A Cup. We went out and showed the Italians how to play. We murdered them.' Ron Yeats recollects, 'Anfield was buzzing, absolutely buzzing. There was steam coming from the Kop. The hair still stands up on the

F A Cup winners 1965.

back of my neck when I talk about the Milan game.'

It's often claimed that football teams are shaped in the image of their manager. Shankly was once quoted as saying, 'My idea was to build Liverpool into a bastion of invincibility. My idea was to conquer the bloody world; and be untouchable. Everyone would have to submit and give in.'

Liverpool's performance against the reigning European champions Inter Milan at Anfield that evening in May 1965 epitomised Shankly's ideals for his team. Roared on by the Kop chant of 'Attack, Attack, Attack', Liverpool tore into Inter and knocked them totally out of their stride. Roger Hunt opened the scoring after only 4 minutes, pouncing on a Callaghan cross to swivel and smash

continued on page 60

THE F A CUP FINAL
1 May 1965

Liverpool	**2**
Leeds	**1** (after extra time)

Edgar Turner of the *Sunday Mirror* described the first 90 minutes thus, 'A match of too many Marlon Brandos and not one Sir Lawrence Olivier. Too much method, not enough individual brilliance.' Sam Leitch, Turner's colleague at the same paper, was even more critical, 'What a Cup final dish to set before the Queen – a blundering ballet of inferior football saved from full stinker status by the first Wembley extra-time for eighteen years.'

The game, indeed, didn't come to life until the extra-time period, when goals from Hunt and St John, with a reply from Bremner, gave Liverpool the F A Cup for the first time in their history.

From the first minutes of the game, it was obvious that the game was going to be a war of attrition. Leeds were determined that Liverpool wouldn't be allowed to settle into their slick passing game, and in the first few minutes their captain Bobby Collins was lectured by the referee for two foul challenges, one of which on Byrne broke the Liverpool full-back's collar bone. The atmosphere on a rain-soaked, grey Wembley day was tense. Goal-scoring chances were sparse and it wasn't until the half-hour mark that either goalkeeper had to make a save.

The second half was once again a dour battle with both sides' defences well on top. Don Revie, the Leeds manager, had obviously hoped that the skill and guile of Collins and the speed of Johanneson on the wing would open the way for a Leeds breakthrough, but both players were virtually anonymous. It wasn't until extra-time that the vigilance of both sides began to loosen, and with tiredness now setting in, the goal chances began to emerge. With 93 minutes gone, the gallant Byrne latched on to a pass from Stevenson and hit a low cross into the centre. Roger Hunt swooped to head the ball home. At last the Liverpool contingent had something to cheer and one joyous fan ran out on to the

pitch to congratulate his heroes. He was immediately pounced on by six policemen, who carted him away feet first. Liverpool's joy was short-lived, however, and Billy Bremner, who had run himself into the ground in Leeds' cause, scored an equaliser 9 minutes later.

Liverpool, who thought they had the Cup won, now had to do it all over again, and it looked like a replay was imminent. With only 9 minutes left to play, the tireless Smith broke from defence to feed Callaghan. The Liverpool winger sped past two Leeds defenders before hitting a low centre that St John headed past Sprake to give Liverpool the Cup.

It may have been a dreary first 90 minutes, but the period of extra-time had been sensational. If ever a result was more important than a display this was it.

Bill Shankly dismissed claims after the game that it had been a dull final. 'I believe this is a terrible exaggeration of what in horse racing terms was a carefully paced middle-distance race, with a thrilling sprint where it counts most – to the finishing post.'

Liverpool's hero of the final, Gerry Byrne, who played for 117 minutes with a fractured collar bone, was called an 'iron-man' by some sections of the press. But the modest Liverpool full-back played down his part in the victory, and told reporters, 'The shoulder didn't trouble me so long as I kept my arm down by my side. I forgot it completely when I made the pass for Roger Hunt to score our first goal.'

Ian St John, whose header won the game, commented, 'I was at the back of the goal near the far post when Ian Callaghan prepared to cross. Then I knew he would drop it short and I went to meet the ball. The goal looked like the Mersey tunnel as I headed in. It was a goal that I will always remember.'

In the Liverpool dressing room after the game, Geoff Strong, who had played so effectively in place of the injured Gordon Milne, took off his shirt and said to Milne, 'Here, Gordon, take my shirt, you are just as much entitled to it as I am.' Although greatly appreciating his team-mate's gesture, Milne would have none of it and shouted back, 'No, Geoff, you keep it, you played in it and you've earned it.'

Leeds manager, Don Revie, acknowledged that the better side had won, a sentiment also expressed by Bobby Collins and Jack Charlton. Leeds' tough, little midfielder, Billy Bremner, cried in the dressing room, as did many of the

Leeds goalkeeper Gary Sprake repels a Liverpool attack.

dejected Leeds team. Bremner said, 'It may only be a game of football but when you lose it seems like the end of the world. When we got back to the dressing room, I wasn't the only one in tears. I wasn't ashamed to cry. But I'm still a kid at twenty-two. I swear I will go back to Wembley again, and I will take home a Cup-Winners' medal.' Bill Shankly, as ever, was already planning for Liverpool's next game, against Inter Milan in the European Cup, and told the press that he intended to frighten the Italians by displaying the Cup to the Anfield faithful before the game. 'We'll bring out the Cup against Inter at Anfield on Tuesday. I think there might be a

noise.' Then, as if the emotion of the day had finally drained Shankly of some of his strength, he looked around at the joyous celebrations that were going on around him and wearily declared, 'What I would like to do now is take a plane directly to Liverpool. You can keep the banquets for me.'

Liverpool: Lawrence, Lawler, Byrne, Strong, Yeats, Stevenson, Callaghan, Hunt, St John, Smith, Thompson

Leeds: Sprake, Reaney, Bell, Bremner, Charlton, Hunter, Giles, Storrie, Peacock, Collins, Johanneson

continued from page 57

the ball into the net. The brilliant Italians hit back almost immediately with Mazzola netting after a sweet Inter move. Liverpool kept to their task and Callaghan put them back into the lead after 34 minutes. For the rest of the game, Liverpool bombarded the Inter goal and were unfortunate to only score one more goal, a St John effort, to take back to Milan.

To beat the European Cup holders 3-1 was still, however, a magnificent effort by the Anfield team. The game has now reached almost legendary status, and to Ian St John it was a milestone in the rise of Shankly's team: 'The Cup final at Wembley drained everybody. To take on the might of Inter Milan was the "night-of-nights". There have been many great nights at Anfield, but I think when people look back, they will say that was the night when Liverpool really came of age.'

Liverpool's demolition of Inter was greeted with a mixture of surprise and acclaim by both the English and Italian press. Many Italian papers admitted that Inter had been lucky to escape with only a 3-1 defeat. One Milan daily wrote, 'Inter were dazed. We lift off our hats to Liverpool. They are a marvellous team.' Another said, 'On the field, Liverpool found all the energies which we thought would be lost after their exhausting battle for the F A Cup. The moving, colourful, picturesque and electrifying support of their fans is not enough to explain the surprising technical quality of their game. The breath of the man who shouts, does not help the man who has to run. It was a miracle, a triumph of athletic soccer; soccer played to win; soccer in which all energies were aimed at the adversary's goal. When a team which understands football in this way wins, the inevitable bitterness of defeat for the Italians is lessened. Soccer played this way belongs to all, everyone would like to see it played this way. For the first time, our world champions felt the earth tremble under their feet and were unable to find sufficient force to react.'

* * *

The return leg in Milan a week later is a game that over thirty years later still arouses anger in the

Liverpool players who participated in it. The atmosphere at Anfield may have been hysterical, but it was nothing to the din that greeted Liverpool when they stepped out onto the San Siro pitch to take in the surroundings before the game began. Ron Yeats claims it was one of Shankly's few mistakes during his managership of Liverpool: 'I think it was one time when Bill slipped up. He took us out on to the pitch and the atmosphere was electric. They were shooting rockets; not into the sky, but down at us on the pitch. It really was frightening.'

Bill Shankly summed it up in a few words. 'It was a war; I've never seen such hostility.'

When Liverpool ran out to face Inter, 90,000 hostile fans greeted them with deafening klaxon horns, smoke bombs and rockets. They were up against it from the word go. Inter Milan were without any shadow of doubt an excellent team and may well have won the tie through playing the excellent football they were capable of, and a series of controversial refereeing decisions went in Inter's favour.

Liverpool's game plan was to soak up early Inter pressure and hit them on the break. Their game plan was in tatters after only ten minutes when they found themselves two goals down; both goals a result of highly debatable refereeing decisions. The first was scored by Corso directly from a free kick that should have been awarded as an indirect. The second was scored by Peiro, who kicked the ball from Tommy Lawrence's hands as he bounced the ball and tapped it into the Liverpool net. The Liverpool players were furious, but the referee waved away all protests and Liverpool were now under considerable pressure not only to stop Inter scoring a third, but to keep their heads over the referee's dubious decisions. With Inter striving for the goal that would take them to the final, the San Siro was now a cauldron of noise.

Inter's European experience was now very much in evidence and after relentless pressure Facchetti scored the winner. As the Liverpool team trooped wearily off the pitch at the end of the game, Tommy Smith admits that he actually assaulted the referee: 'That referee is on my hit list. I've never come

It's ours! The triumphant Liverpool captain Ron Yeats holds the F A Cup for the first time in the club's history.

across him since but I'll admit that as we came off the pitch in Milan, I kicked him. I just booted him and he never changed his step, or even registered that I kicked him. He just kept on walking and I thought, "Yeah, you have been fiddled". Because at the end of the day, he actually should have sent me off, or done something about it. If somebody kicked me, I'd give them a clip back.'

Bill Shankly was furious about the refereeing of the game but refused to lodge a protest. 'Above all things in continental football, you expect to get protection for the goalkeeper. The referee never protected Lawrence in this case and Peiro kicked him on the arm to get possession of the ball. The goal was a disgrace.'

The Italian newspapers were delighted that Inter had reached the European Cup final, but still found time to praise Liverpool. One Milan paper declared, 'Milan has won the most difficult game of its history through a gigantic performance of its defence. Certainly it must have been a torment to play and lose thus, in front of such a public – which undoubtedly surpassed even the madmen of Liverpool.'

The public of Milan went wild that night with Inter fans driving around the city streets waving flags from their cars. One Liverpool fan told the *Liverpool Echo*, 'We couldn't understand what they were saying but crowds of Inter fans were trying to take the mickey. It was peaceful enough, however; no punch-ups followed the game.'

Shankly's dream of leading Liverpool to a unique Cup double was now over, but he had seen nothing in Europe that concerned him. He said, 'In the European Cup you meet cunning, bluff and gimmicks. So much of the continental game is based on the safety first principle, to the detriment of entertainment.'

He wanted to win every game by making the opposition 'submit and give in' but he wouldn't win a European trophy until he reassessed his all-out attack approach in the early 1970s. ●

THE EUROPEAN CUP SEMI-FINAL
Second leg

12 May 1965

Inter Milan	**3**
Liverpool	**0**

As the Liverpool players walked off the San Siro pitch after the most contentious game in the club's history, they were still arguing furiously with Spanish referee Ortiz de Mendibil. The decisions that had angered them had been made over 80 minutes earlier but it was these early decisions that, in the opinion of the Liverpool team, had robbed them of the opportunity of becoming the first British club to reach the European Cup final.

3-1 up from the first leg at Anfield, Liverpool knew they would come under severe pressure from the start. The Italian press had exhorted the Inter fans to make as much of a din as possible. 'Even better than the Beatles' was the request from one paper. The Inter fans did as they were requested and the atmosphere was indeed hysterical, with rockets, smoke bombs and trumpets greeting the Liverpool team's arrival on the pitch.

With five free kicks awarded against them in the opening 5 minutes, Liverpool knew what they were up against from the kick off. As expected, Inter came at them from the start. After 8 minutes, a much disputed free kick was awarded to Inter on the edge of the Liverpool penalty area. Corso took the kick and sent a swerving shot past Lawrence. 90,000 hysterical Inter fans erupted. Just 2 minutes later, Inter scored again with a goal that, even today, is the source of much debate. Tommy Lawrence was bouncing the ball in his penalty area when Peiro sneaked in from behind him and kicked the ball from the astonished goalkeeper's hands before scoring the simplest of goals. The Liverpool players were furious, but the referee allowed the goal to stand.

Liverpool fought bravely to get back into the game, but every time they tackled an Inter player, the referee awarded the Italians a free kick. In the second half, Liverpool continued to push forward for scoring opportunities, but

Inter's well-drilled defence forced the Merseysiders to shoot from long range. There was little doubt that even without the assistance of dubious refereeing decisions, the Italians were a magnificent team, and they proved this emphatically in the 62nd minute. They cut the Liverpool defence to ribbons with a series of quick passes before Corso fed full-back Facchetti, who hammered the ball past Lawrence for Inter's third goal.

After this hammer blow, Liverpool desperately strove for the goal that would level the tie, but they never succeeded in attaining the standard of football that had set the Italian masters back on their heels just a week earlier at Anfield. Inter were happy to play out the final quarter of the game containing Liverpool's increasingly desperate attacking moves. As the final minutes ticked away the Inter fans, mindful of the Kop's taunting of their heroes in the first-leg, chanted 'Addio! Addio!' at the tired and frustrated Liverpool team. At the final whistle, the Liverpool players confronted the referee and jostled him (Tommy Smith took a kick at him) as they left the pitch. The Italian fans began a party that lasted well into the night.

As expected, Bill Shankly was absolutely livid with the referee's performance. 'I have never seen such an appalling display of refereeing. The second goal should never have been allowed. Tommy Lawrence was actually kicked on the hands. It was dreadful.' Lawrence himself remarked, 'As I was bouncing the ball, I received a kick and the next thing I knew, their centre-forward was putting the ball into the net.' Liverpool captain Ron Yeats said, 'I had to go up to the referee at the end. When I saw him taking a bow, I just couldn't restrain myself.'

To have come through this game against an outstanding Inter team to reach the final was always going to be difficult for Liverpool. But to beat the Italians and a dodgy referee, was virtually an impossible task.

Inter Milan: Sarti, Burgnich, Facchetti, Bedin, Guarneri, Picchi, Jair, Mazzola, Peiro, Suarez, Corso

Liverpool: Lawrence, Lawler, Moran, Strong, Yeats, Stevenson, Callaghan, Hunt, St John, Smith, Thompson

Tommy Lawrence sprawls helplessly in the wake of Inter's stunning third goal by Facchetti.

CHAPTER SIX

1965-66

CHAMPIONS AGAIN
The Best Team In England
Since The War

'For years to come dads will be telling their sons, "You should have seen Liverpool in the 1960s. They were the kings of football."'

Sidney Reakes, Liverpool chairman

Shankly and his team with the Championship and Charity Shield trophies in 1966.

Liverpool reported for pre-season training at the beginning of the 1965-66 season, locked in dispute over their request for an increased wage deal. Liverpool's basic wage during the 1960s was amongst the lowest levels in the First Division. Win bonuses and other bonuses based on attendance figures increased their salary, but as F A Cup winners and European Cup semi-finalists, they considered that they had a good case for an increase in their basic wage. A key Liverpool player in the team once remarked, 'If you didn't win you didn't eat.' Ian St John openly admits that the top basic wage he ever received during his ten-year spell at Liverpool was £40 a week. That was in 1971 just before he left the club.

Bill Shankly didn't like to talk money with his players. He was always content with a decent basic wage throughout his career as a player and he thought his players should have the same attitude to the game. Liverpool's current manager, Roy Evans, once asked Shankly if his wages could be

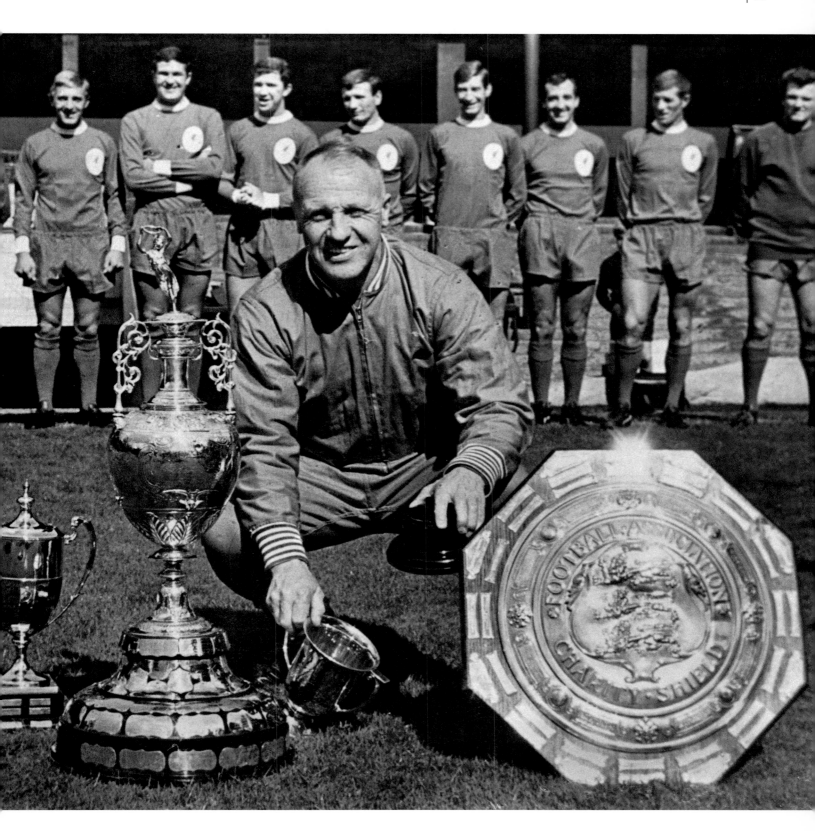

WILLIE STEVENSON

Willie Stevenson had everything that Bill Shankly was looking for in a midfielder – he had a fierce tackle, was a fine passer of a ball and had a good football brain. On top of that he was good in the dressing room, keeping up team morale. The £20,000 Shankly paid Glasgow Rangers for his services in 1962 represented fantastic value.

After taking a little time to adjust to the English game, Stevenson's probing midfield play began to pay dividends, and his partnership with Peter Thompson on the left-hand side was a key factor in Liverpool romping to the League title in 1964. In the F A Cup final the following season, Stevenson was generally acknowledged as Liverpool's key player in a hard-fought final victory over Leeds.

With Championship honours coming Stevenson's way the following season, the talented Scot had picked up three of the games' major honours in just four years with the club. The signing of Emlyn Hughes from Blackpool in 1967 led to Stevenson's departure from Liverpool, and he signed for Stoke City in 1968.

Stevenson ended his football career back on Merseyside with Tranmere Rovers.

increased to £30 a week, and although the Liverpool boss was sympathetic to Evans's request, he still left Shankly's office without his wages increased. A fringe Liverpool player of the 1960s made an impassioned plea to Shankly to increase his wages because his father had recently died and his family was finding it hard to manage. Shankly asked the player if anyone else in his family was working. The Liverpool reserve told his boss that his sister also had a job. 'Tell her to ask her boss for a rise then, you'll not be getting any more money here,' was Shankly's response.

What appears to be a very hard-hearted attitude to his players' requests for better wages is hard to understand. Shankly was the man who on many occasions would take out his wallet and hand over significant sums of money to Liverpool fans who might be stranded far away from home after supporting the team. He would also give financial assistance to Liverpool supporters who were finding it difficult to pay their rent. The Liverpool boss also visited numerous terminally-ill children and their families for days on end helping to get them through probably the most difficult time they would face in their lives. Shankly did all of this and much more for people who were in need of his help.

But when it came to wages, he could be tough. In later years when Tommy Smith was team captain, he asked him to get the rest of the players together and see what the feelings were about a new wage structure. 'You sort it out for me, Tommy,' said Shankly, 'I'll call back later and see what you come up with.' And with that the Liverpool boss left Smith to it. Later that day Shankly returned to find out his players' feelings. Tommy Smith remembers what happened next, 'The players came up with one or two little things. When Shanks came

up to me, I told him I'd had a word with the lads and this is what we suggest. He looked at the list and after each suggestion he said, "No! No! No, son!" He then turned to me and said, "Do yer know what, Smithy, you could cause a riot in a graveyard". He then began to argue with me. I couldn't believe it.'

Ian St John claims that Shankly and his great friend at Manchester United, Sir Matt Busby, both of whom came from a very poor mining background in Scotland, were worried about their players getting involved in spiralling wage increases and that the two of them colluded to keep wages down.

Despite the fact that they weren't among the highest earners in the League, the vast majority of Shankly and Busby's players look back with fond affection on their careers at Liverpool and

Bill Shankly in his office in 1965

Ron Yeats receives treatment during the 1966 local derby at Goodison Park.

Manchester United during the period that these two legends of British football were in charge. 'Shankly played for the love of football and so did we. We just thought we might have got a few bob more,' reflected Ian St John. Shankly did admit to St John in later years that he should have got them better wages.

* * *

Back at the start of the 1965-66 season, however, there was a considerable amount of dissatisfaction at Anfield, and Cliff Lloyd, the secretary of the Players' Association, was called in to assist the Liverpool team in their wage negotiations. Questioned about the dispute, Lloyd told the press, 'I deny as emphatically as possible the rumour being put about that all Liverpool players are seeking a basic wage of £100 per week. Their basic wage, far from being in three figures, has not even been half that sum!'

Bill Shankly said, 'It would be a pity if differences of this sort were to create unease where no uneasiness has existed in the past.'

Sources close to the players claimed that the

Liverpool team were seeking a larger basic wage. If that wasn't forthcoming, they wanted a bonus payment that they considered their performances during the past season deserved. Liverpool's wage dispute dragged on for a few more weeks until the club's Annual Shareholders' meeting on 14 August. It was there that an announcement was made that all of the squad had now signed new contracts for the coming season. Shankly told the shareholders, 'I would like to pay tribute to the chairman, the president and the board for giving the players one of the finest deals I have ever known in the game.'

If Ian St John was only on a £40 per week basic wage six years later in 1971, the deal that had been struck then was obviously still based on bonus incentives.

Shankly went on to talk about his optimism for the coming season, predicting, 'I can't see why we shouldn't win something next year but I won't try to say what it will be. A lot of tension will leave the team because they have already established them-selves as individuals and as a team. Until you get honours, you are always struggling. Now that we have achieved them, we should do even better. Players such as Yeats, Hunt and Byrne are now reaching maturity. They should be at their peak. I reckon a player is best when he is around the twenty-seven mark.'

* * *

As Shankly predicted, Hunt, Yeats and Byrne were once again crucial players in another successful season at Anfield. Roger Hunt, in particular, was in stunning form, and by the time the first Merseyside derby of the season was due in late September, Hunt had already knocked in eight goals.

Prior to the Everton game, Shankly, who lived within yards of Everton's training ground at Bellefield, had been dropping hints that he had been spying on them training from his bedroom window. 'They look absolutely knackered. Harry Catterick has got them running lap after lap around their training ground,' he would say to Bob Paisley, his players only a few yards away, taking in every word. 'Get to the bookies, Bob. Put a few pounds on us, we're going to murder them!'

When Harry Catterick's team arrived at Anfield on the afternoon of the game, Shankly stood in his usual spot at the players' entrance greeting the opposition as they filed past him. Sometimes, he would get one of the Anfield staff to knock on the dressing-room door of the away team and hand them a box of toilet rolls with the words 'Mr Shankly said you'll be needing these'. It was tongue-in-cheek, but as the Liverpool players of the period will confirm, it often did send them out on to the field with a psychological advantage over the opposition.

The famous THIS IS ANFIELD sign over the entrance to the pitch was another Shankly ploy to gain an advantage over the opposition before the game had even began. It told the opposition, once you step past this sign, there is no turning back.

Shankly sent his team out to face Everton in the

'The THIS IS ANFIELD sign was one of Bill Shankly's ideas. Playing at Anfield lifted good pros, but it put the bad ones under pressure. We counted there were more bad pros about than good 'uns, so the sign went up,' said Bob Paisley.

1965 derby feeling that they were about to take on a bunch of leaden-footed geriatrics. Shankly's ploy worked a treat as they thrashed Everton 5-0; the in-form Hunt scoring two.

Shankly would use his brilliant mind and oratorical skills to try to gain an advantage away from the football field as well. At F A disciplinary hearings, he would always try and accompany whichever Liverpool player was appearing: 'He would speak so eloquently and convincingly that members of the commission must have felt that the wrong man had been brought before them!' recalled Ted Croker, who was secretary of the F A during Shankly's period at Liverpool.

The razor-sharp wit of Shankly was never more evident than on one occasion in the late 1960s when one of England's World Cup heroes, Alan Ball, was the idol of the blue half of Merseyside. Alan's father was manager of Preston at the time and contacted Shankly to see if he wanted to accompany him to a mid-week game at Wrexham. The Liverpool boss, always keen to take any opportunity to watch football, agreed to go but said he would follow Alan Ball Snr in his own car to enable him to drive home before the game finished. Shankly was uncertain of the directions to Wrexham, so Ball Snr agreed that Shankly could follow him. When he turned up at Shankly's house, the Liverpool boss was pleased to see that Alan Ball Jnr was in the car with his father. Shankly thought

The men who set a Red Revolution in motion: Bill Shankly, Bob Paisley, Ronnie Moran, Joe Fagan and Reuben Bennett.

PETER THOMPSON

It was Peter Thompson who played a vital role in helping Preston knock Liverpool out of the F A Cup in the 1961-62 season, and Bill Shankly decided there and then that when the opportunity arose, he would take the Carlisle-born wing wizard to Anfield.

A £40,000 fee secured the services of Thompson the following season, though his signing wasn't without incident. He explained, 'When I signed for Liverpool, it was illegal to ask for a signing-on fee. Well, I asked for a signing-on fee and Shanks went white and said to me, "Get out of here. I'm giving you the chance to come and play for the team that is going to become the greatest team in the world; in the greatest city in the world and you're asking for illegal money. Get out of my office!" I said, "Oh all right, give me the pen. I was only joking." So I didn't get a signing-on fee but it was a great thing that I did sign for Liverpool.'

Thompson soon became a Kop idol, with brilliant dribbling skills and ball control. He was to set up many goals for Hunt, St John and others with his pinpoint crossing ability and scored many vital goals himself. One of Thompson's most notable performances was his brace of goals and general all-round display which the Arsenal defence found hard to contain in the 5-0 hammering Liverpool

handed out during their clinching of the League title in April 1964.

Thompson played over 400 times for the Reds before joining Bolton in 1973 and also won 16 England caps during his Liverpool career. He's still fondly remembered by those who had the pleasure of seeing him play.

the world of Ball as a player and would have loved to have brought him to Anfield. When the two cars reached the Mersey Tunnel, Shankly, following a short distance behind Ball Snr, was struggling to keep up and ground to a halt half-way through the tunnel. Shankly may have been a great football manager, but he was renowned for his lack of driving skills and was rather accident-prone. Ball

Snr pulled up and walked back to Shankly, who was struggling to re-start his car. Try as he may, Shankly couldn't get the car to go. 'I tell you what, Bill,' said the concerned Ball Snr, 'I've got a rope in the boot. I'll attach it to your car and tow you to the tunnel exit. We'll then call a mechanic to sort out the problem.' Shankly paused for a few seconds, thinking over Ball Snr's suggestion and then exclaimed, 'I don't think that's a good idea, son. Can you imagine the bloody headlines in tomorrow night's *Echo* if the press find out: 'BILL SHANKLY DRAGGED OUT OF THE MERSEY TUNNEL BY THE BALLS!'

* * *

Whether Shankly managed to get to Wrexham that winter night is unknown, but his Liverpool team were having no difficulty sweeping aside all that came before them during the 1965-66 season. The Christmas holiday period found them facing arch rivals Leeds both at home and away. They lost the first encounter at Anfield, but then travelled to Elland Road the following day and won 1-0. Both were bruising encounters, as Liverpool against Leeds games during this period inevitably were. Tommy Smith said, 'Every time we played Leeds, it was always a battle. Sometimes the football went by the board.'

The *Liverpool Echo* raved about Smith's performance against Leeds during Liverpool's 1-0 victory, proclaiming, 'Smith is a frightening figure as he goes for the ball, with the undoubted intention of obtaining it at any cost. This sturdy young man gives the impression he would cheerfully charge through a brick wall, head first, if he thought it was necessary.'

Their victory over Leeds found the Liverpool team in good heart as they set off across the Pennines for their journey back to Merseyside. Bill Shankly's thoughtfulness when it came to the welfare of the Liverpool supporters was always in evidence during his period at the club, but an incident occurred after the Leeds game that illustrates just what the fans meant to him. The Liverpool team bus had travelled a few miles when Shankly spotted some young Liverpool fans hitch-hiking. 'Pull over,' Shankly ordered the driver when he spotted the teenagers. He opened the coach door and told the surprised fans to climb on board. Space was made for them to sit down. The Liverpool boss then shouted to someone to bring the boys some packs of sandwiches which were always carried for the return journey home: 'There you are, boys, eat them and when you've finished,

go and get your idols' autographs.' The gob-smacked kids must have thought they were in heaven as they looked around them at their heroes they had only ever seen from afar.

After dropping the teenagers off in the city centre, Shankly checked that they had enough money to travel their final distance home. Shankly thought no more of it until one of the boys parents turned up at Anfield the next day to thank him in person for looking after his son. 'It's me, sir, who should be thanking you for allowing your child to support the club. Not you thanking me,' Shankly told the man. When news of gestures such as this spread, it was no wonder that Shankly was rapidly becoming a living legend to the Anfield faithful.

* * *

Liverpool's European Cup Winners' Cup campaign also had started well during the 1965-66 season, particularly when one considers that in the pre-liminary round, they had to take on Italian giants Juventus. The first leg was in Italy and Liverpool did well to hold Juventus to a one-goal defeat. In the return leg, Anfield attendance of 51,000 gave the Italians a hot reception. The Kop serenaded Juventus with a rendition of 'Go Back to Italy' and roars of laughter when the proposed national anthems of both teams failed to materialise as both teams, who were standing in line, looked bemused by the whole event.

The atmosphere was electric, with streams of fainting spectators being stretchered out of the ground for medical attention. When similar scenes of fainting spectators was witnessed by Shankly later in the competition against Celtic, it was little wonder that thoughts were formulating in Shankly's mind that perhaps a move away from Anfield to a bigger venue would be the only answer to the problem of overcrowding at the ground. It would be several years, however, before he would talk to the press about this proposal.

Goals from full-back Chris Lawler, who through-out his Anfield career had a habit of popping up with crucial goals, and Mr Versatility, Geoff Strong, won the tie for Liverpool. Once again, as after the Inter Milan game, the Italian press went crazy over

Phil Chisnall charges in at the Celtic goal during the Celtic v. Liverpool first-leg of the semi-final tie in the in the 1966 European Cup Winners' Cup.

Liverpool and their fans. 'Liverpool were unbeatable tonight, crushing Juventus like almonds in a nutcracker. A pity the cold Juventus fans weren't here to see just how much hot passionate support Anfield gives their team,' raved one Italian paper. Another spoke of Liverpool's football superiority, 'Liverpool gave Juventus a football lesson, playing with vigour and verve. They never once resorted to foul tactics or appeared as if they would get the boot in. The crowd never tried to intimidate Juventus, even if they did sing "Go Back to Italy" to the well-

known "Santa Lucia" tune. The much-feared Anfield crowd showed they are good sports at heart. Juventus were swept aside by Shankly's red devils.'

Further victories against Standard Liege and Honved set Liverpool up for a semi-final clash with Jock Stein's Celtic. The 'Battle of Britain' would prove to be a memorable clash.

* * *

In the League, Liverpool were powering their way to another Championship, including a period in February when they scored four goals in successive

EUROPEAN CUP WINNERS' CUP
19 April 1966

Liverpool	**2**
Celtic	**0**

Although Celtic were officially only allocated 5,000 tickets, it seemed that they had the support of at least three times that number, such was the noise that their supporters made before 'the Battle of Britain' began. For the first time since Shankly's arrival at the club, the Kop were being outshouted. The fact that chants of 'Cel-tic, Cel-tic' from the Scottish contingent was met with the response of 'Go back to Ireland' and 'Rang-ers' by the Liverpool fans added greatly to the pre-match tension. Celtic set out their stall from the start, by deciding not to play talented winger, Jimmy Johnstone, and adopting a defensive approach. They had a one-goal lead from the first leg and were determined to keep it.

The game was played in mud-sapping conditions and from the start, it was a tough, bruising encounter. As expected, Liverpool attacked from the start. Thompson and Callaghan on the wings, sent over a stream of centres and it looked only a matter of time before Liverpool would take the lead. After 30 minutes, Strong sent a pass to full-back Lawler, who was only five yards from goal. Lawler somehow managed to scoop the ball over the bar and the chance was gone. Geoff Strong then sustained a bad injury and was a virtual passenger for the rest of the game. No substitutes were allowed, so he struggled on hoping to make himself as much of a nuisance as possible to the Celtic defence.

The Liverpool breakthrough came in the 60th minute. Tommy Smith, Liverpool's outstanding player on the night, took a free kick. The ball flew through the Celtic defence and Ronnie Simpson in the Celtic goal moved to his right to cover the shot. Somehow the ball evaded him and ended up in the corner of the net. Liverpool bombarded the Celtic goal in their search for the goal that would take them to their first-ever European final. One member of the press described Liverpool's continuous pressure as 'the biggest onslaught

since the days of the Post Office siege in Dublin fifty years ago'. The Liverpool pressure paid off when the injured Strong leapt higher than the Celtic defence to place a Callaghan centre past Simpson. The Liverpool supporters went berserk, with the Celtic fans for the first time that evening lapsing into a deathly hush.

Celtic now had to score themselves to get back into the match, and with 2 minutes of play left, a cross from the wing found Lennox, who swept the ball into the net. The Celtic fans erupted, with their end of the ground a mass of jubilant green and white supporters. Within seconds, their joy had turned to despair when the referee disallowed the goal for offside against Lennox. Bottles, beer cans and other missiles rained down on to the pitch. Photographers, players, police and match officials fled to safety. Celtic trainer, Neil Mochan and physio Bob Rooney bravely ran from their dug-out straight into the danger zone to appeal to the Celtic fans for calm. Rooney was hit on the head by a glass for his troubles, but ignored his injuries as he continued his plea to the Celtic fans to stop the missile attack. Eventually order was restored and the game restarted. After just 30 seconds' more play, the referee blew for time and dashed with the players to the safety of the dressing rooms.

What had been a marvellous game, had ended on a sour and violent note. The Kop chanted 'Hooligans' at the Celtic contingent as the police fought to restore order after the game. The cry of 'Easy, easy, easy' then went up, although beating Jock Stein's talented Celtic team had been far from easy.

Afterwards, Stein was adamant that the referee had cost Celtic the game. 'It wasn't Liverpool who beat us. It was the referee. Bobby Lennox was onside. It was a perfectly good

games against Blackburn, Sunderland and Blackpool; Roger Hunt netting six of them. With the Championship practically ready to enter the Liverpool trophy cabinet yet again, Shankly turned his attention to Celtic and his old pal Jock Stein. 'Celtic were a bloody good side,' recalls Ron Yeats, 'but Shanks had done his homework and we sat back instead of our usual cavalier approach.'

Celtic put Liverpool under intense pressure, but a Bobby Lennox goal was all they had to show for their bombardment of the Liverpool goal. Though unhappy to lose any game, a smiling Shankly told the press that the pitch didn't really suit Liverpool's style. 'I'm quite certain that Jock had got the ground staff to polish it before the game, to help Celtic's chances,' was Shankly's bizarre, but very much tongue-in-cheek, accusation.

Five days later at Anfield, Liverpool attempted to overcome Celtic's one-goal lead in front of a 54,000-plus attendance; their highest home gate of the season and Anfield was full to capacity several hours before kick-off. The Celtic contingent took over the Anfield Road End; many bringing in bottles of liquor. As the game progressed on a damp Merseyside evening, there was the spectacle again of casualties from the Kop having to clamber on to the touchline area to escape the crush. One man suffered a heart attack and an estimated 200 supporters had to receive treatment for minor injuries and fainting. A large proportion of these injuries were sustained when a Celtic goal, that would have levelled the tie, was disallowed for offside. Bottles rained down on to the pitch at the Anfield Road end, many of the missiles damaging Celtic fans at the front of the terrace.

Earlier goals from Smith and Strong won the tie for Liverpool, but Liverpool found themselves in front of the European Football Association for the bottle-throwing incident, and they were issued with the following statement: 'We will warn Liverpool that stern measures will be taken if there is any repetition. The home club are responsible for the conduct of spectators. We also deprecate spectators invading the field with the games being shown on television. Any club

goal,' claimed the man who now enjoys the same legendary status in Glasgow that Shankly does on Merseyside.

Although appalled by the incidents at the very end of the game, the Scottish newspapers were unanimous that Liverpool deserved their victory in what had been a great game. The *Evening Times* was particularly taken by the way that the Celtic fans, until the bottle throwing, had outshone the Kop. It said, 'The flags and banners of this massive army made the red bunting on the Kop look like a cigarette end glowing in the dark – and Celtic fans out-sang, out-shouted, and out-cheered the feared supporters of Liverpool.'

Liverpool: Lawrence, Lawler, Byrne, Milne, Yeats, Stevenson, Strong, Smith, Callaghan, St John, Thompson

Celtic: Simpson, Young, Gemmell, Murdoch, McNeill, Clark, Lennox, McBride, Chalmers, Auld, Hughes

The Kop overflows during the second leg of the European Cup Winners' Cup semi-final against Celtic in 1966. It was scenes such as this that prompted Shankly to think about leaving Anfield for a 100,000 all-seater stadium to be shared with city neighbours Everton at Aintree.

Held scores for Borussia Dortmund in the European Cup Winners' Cup final in 1966; Borussia won 2-1.

responsible for such indiscretions will be firmly dealt with.'

Liverpool, understandably, were furious that their name was tarnished in this way, chairman Sidney Reakes commented, 'It's diabolical. It was the hooligans from Scotland who caused the trouble. The Liverpool fans were first-class.'

During the clean-up of the bottles littering the ground the following morning, it was estimated that over 4,000 bottles had been thrown. At one stage during the incident, the Kop actually began to chant 'Behave Yourselves' to the Celtic fans at the other end of the ground.

Events at Anfield, off the field of play, ensured that the 'Battle of Britain' would be remembered for many years to come (for all the wrong reasons),

but at least Liverpool were now in sight of the first European trophy in their history. Their opponents in the final of the European Cup Winners' Cup were to be Borussia Dortmund and the game would take place at Hampden Park.

Shortly after the Celtic game, Liverpool clinched their second League Championship under Shankly with a 2-1 victory over Chelsea. The Kop were ecstatic, and Chelsea boss, Tommy Docherty, agreed wholeheartedly with Shankly when the Liverpool boss declared after the game that the Anfield faithful were the best supporters in the world, despite the fact that the Kop taunted Docherty's team mercilessly throughout the 90 minutes with chants of 'Show Them the Way to Go Home' and 'London Bridge is Falling Down, Poor Old Chelsea'.

Horace Yates of the *Liverpool Echo* saluted Docherty's team before he too commented on the uniqueness of the Anfield fans, 'Football abounds in this Chelsea outfit and Liverpool could not have wished for more sporting rivals to share these magical moments. They lined up to clap Liverpool on to the field (yes, Ron 'Chopper' Harris was playing!) and it was handshakes all round before they left it.' Turning his attention to the Anfield fans, Yates said, 'Bill is right! There's no football crowd anywhere to compare with the vast Anfield throng for their fervour, their ability to make the most of the occasion, any occasion, great or small, their spontaneous humour and abundant wit. Entirely original, they are not so much part of a scene, as scene-stealers.'

After applauding the Liverpool players as they paraded around a jubilant Anfield, a chant grew louder and louder until the subject of their adulation appeared on the pitch – 'Shankly, Shankly, Shankly' was the cry. Out stepped the Liverpool manager on to the Anfield turf to wave to his adoring army of Anfield fans. They understood entirely the major part that the fanatical Scot had played in the euphoria they were now experiencing.

'To hear the crowd chanting his name, and cheering him puts him in a class apart among managers. I doubt very much if any boss, anywhere in the world, has ever been held in greater esteem – and in saying that, I do not forget the reverence that is felt for Matt Busby at Old Trafford,' said Yates.

Asked about his relationship with the Anfield fans, Shankly replied, 'I'm just one of the people who stands on the Kop. They think the same as I do, and I think the same as they do. It's a kind of marriage of people who like each other.' Chairman Sidney Reakes was overjoyed at yet another success, and aware that perhaps he was witnessing the pinnacle of the present team's achievements he

'Over the season, Liverpool have proved themselves certainly the most consistent of our clubs, as hard as any, but not perhaps as imaginative as some. They are rightly champions at a time when method is valued above flair. Yet, for my liking, Liverpool are still a shade too physical, even in an era of much physical football.'

David Miller in the *Sunday Telegraph* after Liverpool won the League Championship against Chelsea

commented, 'Liverpool are the finest team in Britain and among the greatest club sides I have seen. For years to come dads will be telling their sons, "You should have seen Liverpool in the 1960s. They were the Kings of football."'

It's incredible to note that during Liverpool's successful League campaign of 1965-66, they used only fourteen players, a testimony to Shankly's claims that not only were they the fittest team in the League, but also that they very rarely suffered from injuries.

* * *

With the Championship in the bag, Liverpool now turned their attention to winning their first European trophy. Over 25,000 of their supporters set off for Glasgow in the hope of being present when their team completed an historic double. The match was actually only attended by a 41,000 crowd, with any neutral support that was available from the Scottish contingent going to the German side.

'I could never believe that the neutrals supported the Germans; I'll never forgive them for that!' commented Ron Yeats, still bitter many years after the final. Torrential rain virtually turned the Hampden pitch into a quagmire and this resulted in the game developing into a battle of attrition. Atrocious conditions severely restricted Liverpool's passing style and despite continuous pressure, the disciplined German side took the trophy 2-1 after extra time.

Shankly was bitterly disappointed and refused to give Borussia any credit at all after the game. 'That lot would be hard pushed to hold a place in the English First Division, we were beaten by a team of frightened men. The two goals they scored were flukes,' were just some of Shankly's post match comments. 'It was obviously their plan from the start simply to keep us in subjection,' Shankly went on, 'they had no real attacking plan, but they won, and I am quite sincere when I say that they are the worst team we met in the competition this season.'

EUROPEAN CUP WINNERS' CUP FINAL

5 May 1966

| Borussia Dortmund | 2 |
| Liverpool | 1 |

The Liverpool team arrived back at Speke Airport on Merseyside after this bitter defeat, to be greeted by Liverpool's Lord Mayor and just four supporters. Bill Shankly, however, refused to be downcast and told the waiting press, 'We were beaten by a team of frightened men. They had no real attacking plan. If Tommy Smith and Roger Hunt had been fully fit, we would have won easily.'

Borussia Dortmund may well have not been an outstanding team, but they made up for their lack of skill with a fighting spirit and level of fitness that in many ways mirrored the Anfield team. On the night Liverpool didn't perform to the level they were capable of, and the well organised German team took full advantage.

The game was played in damp, grey conditions and only 41,000 were at the massive Hampden Park ground to witness the proceedings. The game was, in fact, broadcast live on television and this caused much consternation in the press, with the *Daily Mirror* being particularly virulent, branding the live televising of football matches as 'lunacy'. It was claimed in some sections of the media that live broadcasting of games would inevitably lead to falling attendances, and on the night of the Liverpool-Borussia Dortmund final, Arsenal did, in fact, have an end-of-season home game against Leeds, which drew an attendance of only 4,554 to Highbury, their lowest League gate since 1913.

Liverpool, as expected, pressed from the start, with Borussia content to counter-attack after soaking up the pressure. In many ways, their patient style of play was reminiscent of the Liverpool away performances in the 1970s and 1980s that would bring them much success in Europe. As the game progressed, Borussia began to display their own attacking credentials and if the ever dependable Ron Yeats hadn't been having his usual solid game in defence, may even have taken the initiative before half-time.

Borussia finally took the lead in the 62nd minute. Emmerich hit a ball over Yeats to the attacking Held, who was on to the ball like a flash to hit an unstoppable volley past the helpless Lawrence from fully 20 yards away. As usual with Shankly's teams, their heads didn't drop and after a fantastic run from Peter Thompson, who was 40 yards out when he set off in pursuit of goal, he beat three men before crossing to Hunt who hammered the ball into the roof of the net. The German team pleaded with the referee that the ball was out of play when Thompson crossed, but the goal was allowed to stand. After the goal, there was a pitch invasion by hundreds of ecstatic Liverpool supporters, and for a time it looked like the French referee might abandon the game, but the police soon restored order and the game continued.

After a hard-fought 90 minutes, the game went into extra-time. It was Liverpool who now looked the stronger and they mounted wave after wave of attacks at the Borussia defence. After absorbing all that Liverpool could throw at them, Borussia broke away and a long pass from Sturm found Held in acres of space. Held shot, but Lawrence saved bravely, only for the ball to find Libuda 35 yards out. Libuda took aim and curved the ball towards the Liverpool goal. With Lawrence unable to get back into his goal, it was left up to Yeats to clear the danger, but the shot struck a post and then Yeats, who couldn't divert the ball to safety, only succeeded in chesting it across the line. It was a freak goal that had won the day.

The Borussia keeper saves from Roger Hunt.

Despite Shankly's tirade against Borussia, some of his players now acknowledge that when it came to European competition, at least, Shankly was still, at times, tactically naive. Ian St John recently recalled, 'The cavalier attitude that Shanks had wasn't, at the end of the day, going to work for us. We thought there must be a more subtle way. Shanks found it hard to think defensively, he thought teams were going to have an advantage over us if we thought defensively. Shanks' attitude was that we were going to murder everyone. We missed out in the European Cup semi-final and European Cup Winners' Cup final, though I think the players let the management down in that one.'

The Liverpool supporter's reputation for sportsmanship and good behaviour also took a knock after the Borussia defeat. A section of the Liverpool fans booed the German side and several bottles were thrown as they ran their lap of honour. There were also twenty arrests for breach of the peace. Prior to the game, mystery raiders had scaled the Hampden walls in the early hours of the morning and painted the goalposts red. The words 'Liverpool champions' and 'Roger Hunt' were also scrawled in red on the boundary walls by the midnight raiders.　●

After the game, the Borussia Dortmund manager, Herr Malthaup, said, 'We chose to play from behind and it worked.' Bill Shankly shrugged his shoulders and replied, 'We tried to win it, they tried to steal it. They didn't do enough. They were lucky.'

Borussia Dortmund: Tilkowski, Cyliax, Redder, Kurrat, Paul, Assauer, Libuda, Schmidt, Held, Sturm, Emmerich

Liverpool: Lawrence, Lawler, Byrne, Milne, Yeats, Stevenson, Callaghan, Hunt, St John, Smith, Thompson

CHAPTER SEVEN

1966-69

THE BARREN YEARS
So Near And Yet So Far

*'The trouble with you, son,
is that your brains are all in your head
and not your feet.'*

Bill Shankly, to a young Liverpool player

With the exception of Hunt, Callaghan and Byrne, who were on World Cup duty with the England squad, Shankly and the rest of the Liverpool players sat back to enjoy the summer break and the imminent World Cup tournament. Scottish stars Ian St John and Willie Stephenson were invited to make a cameo appearance in the popular BBC sitcom *Till Death Us Do Part*. Merseyside was on a football high with Everton completing a Scouse monopoly of English football's domestic honours by taking the F A Cup after a thrilling final against Sheffield Wednesday. Shankly once declared that Merseyside football fans deserved only the best; 1966 was the year when they got just that.

Everton boss, Harry Catterick, was a great manager in his own right, with two Championships and an F A Cup victory to his credit. Catterick would often get irritable about Shankly's ability to use the press and media to his own and Liverpool's advantage, and once angrily exclaimed, 'It's not my fault if I haven't got a voice like Rob Roy!' in answer to a probing question about his Scottish adversary across Stanley Park at

Geoff Strong in action against Ferencvaros, Anfield 1968.

Anfield. Quite soon after his retirement from football, Shankly invariably received a standing ovation from Evertonians if he was spotted at Goodison Park. This was a unique phenomenon indeed, comparable to Alex Ferguson receiving an ovation at Manchester City.

Shankly once proclaimed that he'd be proud to be called a Scouser. It wasn't said for effect, he meant it. Whether Red or Blue, the people of Merseyside knew Shankly's tribute applied to all of them and they never forgot this.

With Liverpool's Championship victory and Everton's F A Cup triumph, the success of England in the World Cup meant that for Merseyside football fans that year will probably be at the zenith of their football memories.

One man not impressed with the World Cup, however, was Shankly himself; he had always maintained that there was nothing to fear from the rest of the world and was pleased that England had taken the trophy, but he found the standard of play during the tournament sterile and lacking in passion: 'It proved to me that if English clubs wanted to play the continentals at their own defensive game, we would beat them, Liverpool included. But would English fans pay to watch that kind of football every week? In general, I thought the World Cup was played in a negative sense and England won with negative football!'

To Shankly, who had just presided over a Liverpool team winning the title by playing entertaining attacking football for the full 90 minutes, the way one achieved success was as important as the victory itself. He once said, 'There's only two ways to play football, the right way and the wrong way.'

World Champions or not, the only way that Shankly wanted his teams to play was in an entertaining and attacking way, and his two great friends Sir Matt Busby and Jock Stein were of a like mind. In today's football, where the right result takes precedence above anything else in the game

> ### 'If Everton were playing down at the bottom of the garden, I'd draw the curtains.'
> Bill Shankly

because of the vast amount of finance at stake, Shankly, Busby and Stein would have understood why there was the media euphoria after England's dull 0-0 draw against a substandard Italian team in Rome, but they would have been saddened and left cold by what now constitutes a great performance.

Whether Shankly enjoyed the World Cup or not, English football was on a high when the 1966-67 season began, and he reiterated that there was nothing to be learnt from the World Cup. He told the local press, 'We have watched these World Cup teams play and watched them training. But don't think we are going to copy any of their methods. We will prepare and train in the way we've always done, in a manner best suited to our players.'

Ron Yeats said he was certain Liverpool would win another trophy, 'I don't know what, but I hope it will be the European Cup.'

But unbelievably, Shankly's first great team had peaked, and Liverpool were destined to wait another six seasons before they would win another major honour.

* * *

The annual curtain-raiser to the new season, the Charity Shield, saw Liverpool at Goodison Park to take on neighbours Everton. Roger Hunt and Ray Wilson, both members of England's successful World Cup team paraded the trophy in front of 63,000 triumphant Merseysiders. Liverpool won the trophy with a goal from Roger Hunt, and a successful season was anticipated by all at Anfield.

They started well enough with a victory over Leicester, but defeats at Manchester City and an Alan Ball-rejuvenated Everton set them back. There were also problems for them off the field of play after the club decided to ban television cameras from the ground. Liverpool had decided to enforce the ban after fears that television coverage would lead to falling attendances. Everton had also imposed a television black-out at Goodison Park.

Liverpool fans were furious at the club's

Roger Hunt and Ray Wilson, members of the victorious England team, parade the World Cup around Goodison Park before the 1966 Charity Shield game between Everton and Liverpool.

decision. Many of them had difficulties getting into Anfield as it was on big match days; the gates usually being shut well before kick-off time. Petitions against the television ban were organised throughout the city, one in particular from close on 10,000 workers at the Ford car factory stating that unless the ban was lifted, then supporters would be encouraged to boycott all Liverpool matches. One irate fan proclaimed, 'This is ridiculous. It's something I didn't expect from Liverpool. We have yet to hear a plausible reason from the club for their attitude – the old excuse about dwindling crowds just won't do. The opposite is the case at Anfield. It will be difficult for me and the other Liverpool supporters at the plant to stay away but it will show how strongly we feel about it.'

Liverpool's growing band of supporters from outside the Merseyside area were particularly enraged by not being able to see their heroes on television and sent letters of protest to the *Liverpool Echo*. One stated, 'I hope that for the sake of exiled supporters like myself, the club will reconsider this decision. So far as I can judge, outside the Merseyside area, Liverpool aren't considered a great team. They aren't, as I think they should be, compared with Busby's team of the late 1940s and mid 1950s. Nor the Spurs double-winning team, or even Wolves, England's first conquerors of top-class European competition. To gain this deserved reputation, Liverpool need the medium of TV, for after all, there is as much satisfaction to be gained from national recognition as that given by local fans.'

This staunch display of 'people power' caused the Liverpool board to re-think their decision, and the ban on television cameras was lifted. With a televised thrashing at the hands of Ajax only weeks away, however, perhaps the powers that be at Anfield wished they had enforced the ban a short while longer!

* * *

Shankly had every reason to feel confident that Liverpool would have a major part to play in that season's European Cup. He had always maintained that a player is at his best when he is twenty-seven or twenty-eight years old. With many of his squad

THE F A CHARITY SHIELD
13 August 1966

Everton	**0**
Liverpool	**1**

After this game, soccer great Joe Mercer declared, 'For the first time in years, I've seen a team which I wasn't good enough to play in.' Liverpool totally outplayed Everton and the general consensus of those present was that Liverpool should have won by at least four clear goals.

The day began with the unique sight of the F A Cup, League Championship trophy and World Cup all being paraded around Goodison Park, a ceremony unlikely to ever be repeated. Liverpool's goal came after just 9 minutes. Brilliant interchanging, between Hunt, Callaghan and Thompson set up the chance, which Hunt blasted into the top corner from 20 yards out. A glut of goals looked on the cards as Liverpool ran a despondent Everton team ragged. Roger Hunt, who was captain for the day, looked outstanding as chances were set up by the tireless Ian Callaghan and scintillating Peter Thompson on the other wing. The fact that Liverpool failed to put the gloss of their undoubted superiority on their performance with more goals would haunt them throughout the coming season.

In attack, Shankly decided to play Strong alongside Hunt, with St John linking up with Liverpool's midfield. Unsettled Gordon Milne was the man to miss out and speculation was mounting that a transfer request was imminent. After this display, it looked difficult for Shankly to make changes for the opening game of the season. Throughout the match, Liverpool looked in total control with each of their players on top of their game. Particularly outstanding were the Liverpool contingent who had been on World Cup duty with England's triumphant squad. Hunt, Callaghan and Byrne all had outstanding games, with Gerry Byrne at times looking more like England's left-back than the current occupier of that position, Everton's Ray Wilson.

Towards the end of the game, Liverpool stroked the ball about with what was described by one soccer pundit as 'machine-gun accuracy'. Everton looked totally bewildered and were even jeered by their own supporters. Koppites in the crowd sang 'Show them the way to go home, they're tired and they want to go to bed', and chanted 'How did they win the Cup?' The banter was, as usual, good natured, and Evertonians joined Liverpool fans in applauding Liverpool as they paraded around Goodison

**Colin Harvey tackles
Roger Hunt in the 1966
Charity Shield game.**

at the end of the game with the Charity Shield.

After the game, Bill Shankly told the press that he was satisfied with the Liverpool display and singled out Ian St John for particular praise. 'He has no equal at that sort of game. He didn't put a foot wrong as our midfield link man,' said the Liverpool chief, who at this stage in the season refused to take any notice of press predictions that there was no team in the First Division capable of stopping Liverpool retaining the Championship. Most of the 63,329 who

witnessed this tremendous display, however, left Goodison Park agreeing with the soccer media that Liverpool would take some stopping in the new season.

Everton: West, Wright, Wilson, Gabriel, Labone, Glover, Scott, Trebilcock, Young, Harvey, Temple

Liverpool: Lawrence, Lawler, Byrne, Smith, Yeats, Stevenson, Callaghan, Hunt, St John, Strong, Thompson

Banter in the director's box at Anfield during a Manchester United visit. Throughout the Shankly era at Liverpool, Manchester United backroom staff and players were among Shankly's closest football friends. The current bitter rivalry between the two sets of supporters would probably have left him puzzled and sad.

fitting into this category, Shankly's first great team should have been at their peak, but Liverpool started their campaign nervously. They had to get past Romanian champions Petrolul Ploesti in the preliminary round. They won the first leg at Anfield 2-0, but lost 3-1 in the return. A third game was needed and Liverpool, through goals from St John and Thompson, won a place in the next round.

They were drawn to meet Dutch champions Ajax next and not too many problems were anticipated. Dutch football wasn't regarded as particularly strong, and Liverpool fans had more fun joking about the name of the Dutch champions, which was the same as a well-known brand of toilet cleaner. After Liverpool's humiliation at the hands of the Dutch team, Evertonians had fun at the expense of Liverpool for years to come with jibes like, 'How do you flush Liverpool down the toilet? Sprinkle them with Ajax!'

One of Liverpool's concerns before the game was the part, if any, that a nihilistic group who were causing the Dutch authorities a lot of concern,

would play. During a recent international match between Holland and Czechoslovakia, the 'Provos', as the nihilists called themselves, had invaded the playing area and fought with the police and other fans. As a result, the pitch at the Olympic Stadium, where the Liverpool game would take place, was barricaded with coils of barbed wire. As it turned out, the only pitch invader that dank, foggy night was Shankly himself. Another precaution taken by the Dutch authorities was a 100-foot tunnel of unbreakable glass to prevent the players being hit by bottles when the players walked out on to the pitch. Although the Ajax club claimed it wasn't their supporters who were to blame for the recent trouble at the ground, the authorities were taking no chances and an ultimatum was issued to them that if there was any more trouble, football would no longer be allowed at the Olympic Stadium.

On the night of the game, a fog descended on Amsterdam and Shankly argued with match officials that the game should be called off. Shankly's pleas were to no avail and the game went ahead.

JOHN TOSHACK

Cardiff-born John Toshack signed for Liverpool from Cardiff City in 1970. His fee was £110,000, and he quickly became a Kop favourite after taking Liverpool to a 3-2 victory over Everton, who had been leading 2-0 at one stage. The partnership that Toshack was to form with Kevin Keegan has taken on legendary status, and there were even claims at one stage that the two of them were telepathic.

Already an established Welsh international when he signed for the club, Toshack was to take his tally to 40 international appearances before he retired from the game.

Toshack's first major game for the club was the F A Cup final in 1971 against Arsenal. He revealed in his autobiography that Shankly, on the eve of the final, took them to a show at the London Palladium. They were taken to meet the star of the show, comedian Tommy Cooper, backstage and Shankly was astounded at the size of Tommy's feet: 'Jesus Christ, son, what size shoes are they? I've sailed to Ireland in smaller boats than that!' Shankly enquired of the entertainer. Liverpool lost the final, but Toshack and his team would achieve much success over the next few years.

Bob Paisley once said of Toshack, 'Sometimes I wonder how good he might have been but for a niggling run of thigh injuries. He was certainly a far more accomplished player than his critics claimed and he had relatively finely tuned skills for such a big man.'

Toshack left Liverpool in 1977 to take up the offer of becoming player/manager at Swansea, and within five seasons, had led them from the Fourth Division to the First.

THE EUROPEAN CUP
7 December 1966

| Ajax | 5 |
| Liverpool | 1 |

With the Ajax supporters chanting 'Ha-Ha, Liverpool' throughout, at the end of the game, Liverpool's greatest humiliation in Europe was complete. The result shocked European football to the core. How could this happen to the team who had acquitted themselves so well in their previous European campaigns? The answer lay in the fact that Liverpool gave their most inept defensive display in years against an outstanding Ajax attack of Cruyff, Nuninga and Swart. Ajax created five clear-cut chances and took all of them.

The match had been in doubt all day, with fog looking likely to cause a postponement. The Italian referee, Mr Shadella, considered that although the fans couldn't see, the players could. So the game went ahead. But although the 65,000 present didn't know what was going on, they certainly made themselves heard.

The goal scoring began as early as the 3rd minute, with De Wolf, playing his first game for the club, opening the scoring. After 17 minutes Cruyff scored Ajax's second after a skirmish in the Liverpool goalmouth. One reporter described Ajax as 'the white-shirted Dutchmen flitting like ghosts through the mist and through the defence of Liverpool'.

With 30 minutes gone, Bob Paisley went on to the pitch to attend to an injured Liverpool player. Bill Shankly followed Paisley out on to the pitch that was now shrouded in fog again and began to issue instructions to his beleaguered players, but was eventually spotted by an official and ordered from the field of play. The message from Shankly was obviously to get stuck in in an attempt to throw the Ajax team off their game. The foul count against Liverpool began to mount and Suurbier was taken off with a damaged ankle. Tommy Smith then charged down Cruyff on the edge of the penalty area. From the resulting free kick, Nuninga scored a third after Liverpool failed to get the ball away. Ajax were now rampant and Nuninga added a fourth just before the half-time break. The Ajax supporters were now delirious. Before the game, Liverpool were regarded as one of Europe's best – this reputation was now in tatters.

After the break, Liverpool came at Ajax with a vengeance in an attempt to claw back the goal deficit. Ajax drew every man back into defence, and then, with the visibility receding by the minute, Ajax pulled away and Groot scored Ajax's fifth goal with just 16 minutes left to play. Later that evening, when television showed highlights of the game, Liverpool fans back on Merseyside sat open-mouthed, unable to take in what they were seeing.

One of those fans was Steve Coppell, later to find fame with Manchester United and England. 'I was with a group of fellow Liverpool fans huddled around a crackling radio with fading batteries. When the result came through, Ajax 5 Liverpool 1 – surely not. It must have been a mistake. Liverpool never lost 5-1 to anybody. What would Shankly say? The next morning, the newspapers revealed the thoughts of the great man. Liverpool were beaten by the fog! The Dutch were used to playing in the fog and that explained the result.'

The Ajax goalkeeper saves as St John challenges in the first leg of the 1966 European Cup.

The ever-optimistic Shankly really did believe that all wasn't lost. He told one reporter, 'This tie is by no means over yet. We will win easily. We will smash in at least seven goals. This was ridiculous. Ajax played defensive football on their own ground.'

This was one occasion, however, when Shankly's men had left themselves with an insurmountable mountain to climb.

Ajax: Bals, Suurbier, Pronk, Soetckouw, van Duivenbode, Groot, Muller, Swart, Cruyff, Nuninga, de Wolf

Liverpool: Lawrence, Lawler, Smith, Yeats, Stevenson, Callaghan, St John, Strong, Hunt, Graham, Thompson

Visibility was, in fact, so poor that Shankly at one stage wandered on to the pitch to issue instructions to his players. 'You couldn't see the game at all,' he said. 'I was on the pitch. We were 2-0 down, so I went out on to the pitch to have a word with my players and the referee never even saw me.'

Liverpool ended up being beaten 5-1, and although the conditions made the game farcical, there was no doubting that Ajax contained some outstanding talent; notably nineteen-year-old future soccer legend Johann Cruyff.

As expected, Shankly was furious after the game. 'We never play well against defensive teams!' he told the incredulous press.

Remarkably, Shankly convinced the Liverpool supporters that the four-goal deficit could be overcome and close on 54,000 packed into Anfield in the hope of witnessing one of the greatest comebacks of all time.

Despite the fact that Shankly had branded them a defensive team, Ajax manager, Rinus Michels, told the press that he wasn't impressed with the Liverpool defence and expected to score more goals. Dutch wonderboy Cruyff was ill for several games before the return leg, but was passed fit to play.

Roared on by the Kop, Liverpool swept forward from the start, but were unable to take an early lead. There was the surreal sight of smoke rising from the Kop, and, once again, the all too familiar spectacle of crushed spectators spilling down on to the side of the pitch. A panic ensued and there was even reports of a smoke bomb being set off. Thirty were taken to hospital and over 100 were treated by ambulance services at the ground. A police spokesman told the *Liverpool Echo*, 'You could feel the terrific excitement and tension at the beginning of the match and the pressure from the top of the Kop was probably greater than it usually is.' The crush happened 20 minutes into the match and by half-time, the anticipated Liverpool breakthrough had failed to materialise. Two goals from Cruyff; Liverpool responding with a Hunt double, led to Ajax winning the tie 7-3 on aggregate. Roger Hunt was later to claim, 'Little was known about Ajax in those days, but they were a far better side

Emlyn Hughes, Tommy Smith and Peter Thompson go to join the England squad in the late 1960s.

than we imagined.' Tommy Smith, as usual, was more forthright, 'Ajax were a great side!' Shankly was still reluctant to praise the rapidly emerging Dutch masters of European football; 'They were lucky,' he exclaimed.

* * *

In the Football League, the expected retention of the championship was also not going Liverpool's way, with a George Best-inspired Manchester United sweeping all before them as they went on to take their second title in two seasons. The F A Cup was also out of Liverpool's reach, an Alan Ball goal putting Everton into the next round at the expense of their city rivals.

Shankly had always fiercely rejected any criticism of his team, but new blood was obviously needed

to rejuvenate his squad. He had been tracking Blackpool youngster Emlyn Hughes for several months, after witnessing Hughes's debut for the Lancashire club, and was determined to sign him. He had even taken to phoning Hughes on a Sunday morning to tell the youngster that he'd be a Liverpool player soon: 'I'd be just about to make short work of a plate of eggs, bacon and black pudding when the phone would ring. It would be Shanks. "Hey, Emlyn son, don't eat that stuff you've got on your plate there. I'll be signing you shortly. I want you lean and hungry, son. Lean and hungry!" Today, thirty years later, I still associate the smell of bacon frying with the telephone ringing at 8.30 sharp on a Sunday morning,' said Hughes.

Emlyn Hughes would prove to be one of Shankly's key signings as the successful Liverpool team of the 1960s began to disband. He also attempted to sign another emerging youngster, Howard Kendall, from Preston. But Preston had already sold Gordon Milne, Peter Thompson and David Wilson to Liverpool and the Deep Dale fans had taken to chanting 'Stay away Shankly' when he was spotted at the ground. Kendall ended up being sold to Everton and Shankly was furious that he hadn't been given the opportunity to put in his bid for the player.

During the summer months of 1967, Shankly decided to splash out again and paid £96,000, a considerable sum at the time, for Chelsea's formidable centre-forward Tony Hateley. Chairman Sidney Reakes was as hungry as Shankly to win more trophies and was ready to come up with whatever money was needed to achieve success. He said, 'At Anfield, we don't live on memories. What has been done is history and now we are as eager as ever to begin the writing of new pages. We are poised and ready to move just as soon as the market throws up the type of reinforcement we need.' Shankly reiterated his chairman's desire for further success, 'The Liverpool public have been weaned on success. Anything less would be insult to them.'

Liverpool were actually well placed to regain the League title until the beginning of March. But only two victories in the final eleven games allowed

EMLYN HUGHES

Bill Shankly signed Emlyn Hughes to replace
Willie Stevenson in the Liverpool team.
Hughes, who cost the Reds £65,000 from
Blackpool in 1966, turned out to be one of
the key signings in Shankly's managerial
career at the club.

'I knew he was a winner,' Shankly later
said of the player that the Kop were to dub
'Crazy Horse'. 'There are some players you go
to watch and you really think they can play,
but you're not too sure. I knew with Emlyn
Hughes there was no risk.'

The dynamic performances of Hughes in
the Liverpool midfield, soon brought him
national recognition, and he won the first of
62 England caps in 1969.

Hughes was just as adept in a defensive
role, and with Phil Thompson, formed an
outstanding partnership in the centre of
Liverpool's defence during the club's golden
period of success in the 1970s. Hughes
played 657 times for Liverpool and captained
their first European Cup-winning side in 1977.

Legend has it that Bill Shankly
prophetically told a police officer, who had
stopped Shankly for having faulty rear lights
on his car, 'Don't you know who is in this
car?' (Shankly was taking Hughes back to
Anfield to sign for the Reds.) When the
bemused policeman said he didn't, Shankly
exclaimed, 'There sits the future captain of
England!' As usual, Shankly's prophecy was
to prove correct.

Emlyn Hughes, a key
player in Shankly's
second great team, went
on to be the first Liverpool
captain to hold the
European Cup.

Manchester United to pull away. The meagre eight goals scored in that eleven-game sequence was enough to tell Shankly that more fire power was needed up front.

* * *

Everybody at Anfield, at the beginning of the 1967-68 season, anticipated that Tony Hateley would provide the much needed goals to enable Liverpool to take the title again. He started his Anfield career well enough, with a hat-trick in his third game, a 6-0 drubbing of Newcastle. It would be the darling of the Kop, Roger Hunt, however, who would still provide the bulk of Liverpool's goals. To accommodate Hateley, Liverpool changed their style of play from their quick passing game to a more direct method, getting the ball out quickly to the wing for Callaghan or Thompson to whip over crosses. It was hoped that the formidable heading ability of

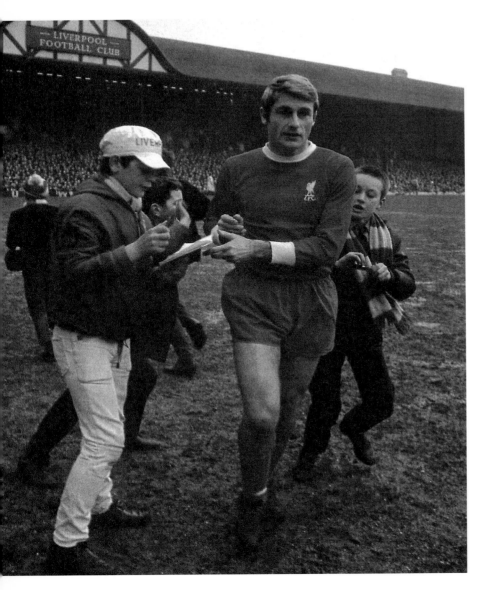

Roger Hunt autographs a young Liverpool fan's programme during the late 1960s at Anfield.

away, Liverpool agreed to a 1.00 kick off to enable them to fly back to Liverpool directly after the game.

They did well to hold the talented Hungarians to a 1–0 defeat, but after the game, Shankly disputed the goal and condemned the referee, 'When the ball was centred that led to their goal, it was at least two feet out of play; and when we made a tackle, it was a free kick. The Italian referee wouldn't allow physical contact.'

Shankly was confident that Liverpool would beat the Hungarians at Anfield and win through to the next round, but first there was another hazardous journey back to Liverpool to contend with. The general consensus is that throughout the Shankly era, the Liverpool boss disliked the long treks abroad and hated flying in particular. The flight home from Budapest was another nail-biting affair. The Liverpool squad had to stay sealed in their plane while ground crew cleared snow, ice and slush from the runway. The wings of the aircraft then had to be de-iced in a snow blizzard before an attempted take off was possible. Thankfully, the plane was able to depart during its first attempt. While in mid air, Shankly, now in a more relaxed frame of mind, was informed that it had been touch and go as to whether the airport was going to have to be closed due to the hazardous conditions. At times like this, it was no wonder that the Liverpool manager would ask himself if football really was more important than life and death.

In the return leg at Anfield, Ferencvaros took an early lead and held out to take the tie 2-0 on aggregate. Europe had once again proved to be Shankly's Achilles heel. Leeds United, by now an outstanding team, actually went on to beat Ferencvaros in the final of the Fairs Cup towards the end of the 1967-68 season. Shankly would have to wait several more seasons before his team would triumph in Europe.

* * *

Liverpool ended their League programme in third place to Joe Mercer's Manchester City. A re-think was clearly needed if Liverpool were to Challenge for the game's top honours again.

Hateley would net him a bagful of goals, but the plan never really succeeded.

In the Inter Cities Fairs Cup, Liverpool began their campaign well enough, with victories over Malmo and TSV Munchen. In the next round, they were drawn against Hungarian team Ferencvaros, who had just won their domestic League Championship with twenty-four victories in twenty-seven games. Ferencvaros also included nine of the current Hungarian team in their line-up. The first leg was due to be played in Hungary. With the onset of the harsh Hungarian winter only days

Although no trophies came Liverpool's way in 1968, their balance sheet for the season was showing a healthy profit. Gate receipts alone brought in £395,000, with Liverpool being the third best-supported team in the country behind Manchester United and Everton.

Shankly knew that money would be available to strengthen the team and in September he decided to make Wolves promising youngster, Alun Evans, his boldest signing to date. Evans cost £100,000, a record fee for a teenager. Part of this money had been recouped a few weeks earlier by off-loading Tony Hateley to Coventry for £80,000.

Apart from rebuilding his team, Shankly had other things on his mind during the summer of 1968. The welfare of Liverpool's supporters was always uppermost in his thoughts, and although, since his arrival at Liverpool in 1959, there had been major improvements at the ground, to Shankly it was still not good enough for the Anfield faithful. The Kop was a unique phenomenon, and created an atmosphere that couldn't be bettered anywhere in the world. But the sight of crushed fans, laid out on the side of the pitch, gasping for breath, had occurred all too often, particularly during big match nights in Europe, for Shankly's taste.

The Liverpool boss began to make noises about the unthinkable – Liverpool moving from their beloved Anfield. For a long time, residents who lived near to Anfield, in the narrow streets that surrounded the ground, had been resentful about being virtual prisoners in their own homes on match days. There were even reports in the press of violent clashes between residents and Liverpool fans before and after the game. Much of the aggravation was caused by fans queuing to get in.

Hunt races towards the Ferencvaros goal during Liverpool's European Fairs Cup tie at Anfield in 1968.

RAY CLEMENCE

Ray Clemence joined Liverpool from Scunthorpe in 1967. The first person he met when he arrived at Anfield was Bill Shankly himself: 'Shanks proceeded to show me around every piece of Anfield, including the toilets. He then took me on to the pitch and showed me the Kop. He explained that you could be playing in front of the best set of fans in the world. Then you were taken to Melwood to see the training ground. By the time he'd finished all that, you weren't even talking about finance, you just wanted the contract to put your name on it.'

Liverpool signed probably the best goalkeeper in their history for just £18,000. Clemence had to wait another two seasons before taking over from the consistent Tommy Lawrence. After that Clemence went on to make 656 appearances for the Reds. His consistency was crucial to the construction of Shankly's second great team in the 1970s, and the Liverpool manager once remarked, 'Ray Clemence could possibly be the greatest factor in Liverpool's success of all because of the things he does as a goalkeeper. The goals he's saved in a season that may have sneaked in. This changed the whole course of a game.'

When it came to international honours, Clemence was unlucky to be in competition with the equally outstanding Peter Shilton, although he still managed to win 61 England caps in his long illustrious career. By the time Clemence joined Spurs in 1981, the haul of honours that he had won at Anfield included: 3 European Cup winners' medals, 1 UEFA Cup winners' medal, 5 League Championship medals, 1 F A Cup winners' medal and 1 League Cup winners' medal.

Apart from his medal haul, probably Clemence's greatest season at the club was in 1978-79, when incredibly he let in just 16 League goals all season.

One resident of Kemlyn Road told the local press, 'There's no good will at all for Liverpool F C in the roads round the ground. For too long the club has walked with hob-nailed boots over the residents. This can't go on any longer and we are asking the Chief Constable to protect the district.' Another resident stated, 'I'm a great fan of Liverpool and love to see them win, but I don't go to matches any more because of the discomfort and rowdyism. If any other private company treated residents in a similar way, they would be have been prosecuted long ago.' What upset the residents the most was the foul language and their passageways being used as public conveniences.

From the club and Shankly's point of view, there was also the fact that on many occasions, particularly for big matches, the gates were locked at Anfield well before kick-off time. The ground simply wasn't big enough for the growing number of supporters who wanted to watch Liverpool, and this meant that potential revenue was lost to the club. With all of these factors in mind, it was no wonder that Shankly was thinking hard about the possibility of leaving Anfield.

'I would far rather stay at Anfield of course,' he told the *Daily Post*. 'If only we could provide seats for 40,000, what a ground that would be, with its unmatched atmosphere. But the comfort of our followers is something which concerns me deeply. These people, who are prepared to stand in all weather throughout the season in all manner of climatic trials deserve a reward. They deserve a seat.' He even told the interviewer where a new stadium could be situated, 'If we could build a 100,000-seater stadium at Aintree; to be shared with Everton, then I would be tempted to move from Anfield.'

After the Hillsborough tragedy, Liverpool, of course, did turn Anfield into an all-seater stadium. But it's interesting to note that way back in 1968, the visionary Shankly, with the safety and comfort of his beloved Liverpool supporters in mind, was prepared to contemplate an exodus from Anfield to share a new stadium with city rivals Everton.

* * *

One place that had been drastically improved since Shankly's arrival in 1959 was Liverpool's training headquarters at Melwood. There was now a new pavilion, treatment room, saunas and an all-weather pitch equipped with floodlights. Back in 1959, there hadn't even been running water available.

Welcoming his squad back for pre-season training, Shankly gave a warm reception to the new group of youth players that had joined the club. 'You have joined a great club with the finest traditions,' he said. 'Here we have no interest in politics or religion. It doesn't matter what you are so long as you can play football. The Liverpool club success has been based on hard work and simplicity. That

'Some people regard me as a callous, ruthless individual. How wrong they are! I'm first and foremost a player's man. If I think a player is entitled to something I won't rest until he gets it. I believe in giving him a square deal, but in return I demand nothing less than that!' said Bill Shankly.

Roger Hunt evades the tackle of Ron 'Chopper' Harris to score against Chelsea; this goal in 1969 set a new Liverpool League goal-scoring record of 233 goals. Bill Shankly said, 'Roger Hunt was a brilliant player. He could leather them, or he could score with a simple tap-in or a nod of the head. But he much preferred to batter them in – he liked to make sure.'

is the motto here and it will continue to be so.' He concluded his pep talk by telling the youngsters not to be afraid to ask the senior players for help and advice. 'Don't hesitate to approach the players,' he told them. 'They know all the answers. These men have been among the most successful players in Britain for the last six years. They know the game. Talk to them.'

Not all of the youths at Liverpool during the Shankly years, however, were won over by the Scot's fanatical style of management. Paul Fairclough, the manager of non-League Stevenage during their headline-grabbing F A Cup run of 1997-98 season, was a sixteen-year-old member of Liverpool's C team during the mid 1960s. After one defeat, Shankly was livid and burst into the dressing room to tell the youngsters what he thought of them. Fairclough recalled, 'He strode in, thumped the desk, smashed a cup and came round criticising each one of us close to our faces. When he got to

me, I just laughed out loud because I thought he was a madman. He went totally ballistic. I just couldn't take on board this man getting so worked up about football. I'd love to say I got swept along with the Shankly era at Liverpool, but really I can't say I learned anything. It's quite sad but I didn't.'

* * *

The 1968-69 season began slowly for Liverpool with three victories in their first seven games. The introduction of Alun Evans into the team in September, however, coincided with Liverpool stepping up a gear. They won five games in succession, scoring eighteen goals and conceding none in the process. Evans looked destined to become the new idol of Anfield. In Europe in-form Liverpool were confident they could overcome top Spanish club Atletico Bilbao in the Fairs Cup. The first leg in Spain resulted in a 2-1 defeat. The return at Anfield saw Liverpool win by the same score. Ron Yeats stepped into the centre circle to decide who would go through on the toss of a coin. The toss went against Liverpool and they went out. After going out of the F A Cup to Leicester, there was only the League to aim for. At one stage in the season, they actually pulled four points clear of eventual champions, Leeds, but an unimpressive run in with only two victories in their last seven games saw Don Revie's team overhaul them on their way to a comfortable title victory.

Liverpool finished without a trophy again. The only crumb of comfort for Shankly was the fact that four players were now at Anfield who would become vital ingredients of his next great team. The recently signed Alec Lindsay, who would be converted from an impressive wing-half into an outstanding full-back, goalkeeper Clemence and mid-fielder Brian Hall who were biding their time waiting for their chance to impress. Centre-half Larry Lloyd had also been snapped up from Bristol Rovers for £50,000, and would eventually take Ron Yeats's place at the heart of the Liverpool defence.

Liverpool go out of the European Fairs Cup on the toss of a coin against Atletico Bilbao in 1968.

CHAPTER EIGHT

1969-73

KEVIN McDAFT
The Final Piece In The Jigsaw

'Bill Shankly made his vision and dreams of Liverpool come true. He put his character into the club in every facet from the bottom to the top.'
Kevin Keegan

Inevitably Shankly's great team of the 1960s began to disband. Players such as Stevenson, Milne and Byrne had already been replaced, and for Lawrence, Strong, Yeats and St John, their Liverpool careers were drawing to a close.

Liverpool began the 1969-70 season in great style, winning their opening four games and not tasting defeat until mid September, away to Manchester United. After that reverse, their results became inconsistent. Roger Hunt and Ian St John struggled to retain their places in the team and discarding them caused Shankly much heart-searching. St John was dropped for an away game at Newcastle and recalls that Shankly was nowhere to be seen when he was told the news, 'Shankly avoided coming into the dressing room until five minutes before the kick off. I'd been his first big signing at the start of the revolution and he couldn't bear to sit down and say to me, "I'm leaving you out." When I asked him why didn't you tell me earlier? He said, "You weren't in the dressing room when I announced the team." He couldn't bear to tell me face-to-face.'

Bob Paisley claimed that Shankly found it hard to hurt players who had served him with distinction. 'If Bill had one failing, it was the fact that he didn't like to upset players that had done so well for him. He was a softie at heart.'

Shankly had always cultivated the 'tough guy' image, but those who knew him well said it was all a myth. Soccer luminary Joe Mercer had known Shankly since the 1930s and had no doubts that the Scot wasn't the hard man that many thought he was. 'They say he's tough, he's hard, he's ruthless. Rubbish, he's got a heart of gold, he loves the game, he loves his fans, he loves his players. He's like an old Collie dog, he doesn't like hurting his sheep.

He'll drive them, certainly, but bite them, never.'

Roger Hunt also found it hard to come to terms with being dropped from the team; the first time being the previous season when Shankly took him off against Leicester. Hunt recalled, 'Ron Yeats approached me and said he thought the management wanted me off. I said words to the effect that they could get stuffed. Then the referee came to me and said I was being called off. I had no choice then. As I passed the bench, I pulled off my shirt and threw it into the dug-out before marching straight inside to have a bath.' Hunt, always the gentleman and a legend at Anfield for as long as Liverpool exists, probably reacted in a way that

Tommy Smith and Alan Ball of Everton lead out their teams for the 1969 Goodison Park derby. Shankly would often phone up Ball to talk football, and Ball once said, 'Shankly was very special. The greatness of the man was the fact that he wasn't frightened to give praise, even if it was to the so-called worst enemy.'

surprised Shankly, but the Liverpool boss definitely didn't want players at the club who showed no reaction to losing their place.

* * *

It was difficult for Shankly, but hard decisions had to be made, and defeat in the F A Cup at Watford was the point of no return for several Liverpool players. Shankly said in later years that key players Tommy Smith and Peter Thompson had been injured for the Watford game, and that those two on their own probably could have beaten the London club. Looking back at the Watford game, he admitted, 'That defeat hastened the break-up of a once-great team. I knew I had to rebuild again. We bought Larry Lloyd, Ray Clemence and Alec Lindsay. We couldn't buy £100,000 players and then put them in the reserves. We had to buy from the lower Leagues to allow them time to play in the reserves. They were happy to come to Liverpool and learn their trade.'

Liverpool ended the season in fifth position, fifteen points behind champions Everton.

* * *

Billy Bremner heads at goal during the European Fairs Cup tie at Anfield in 1971.

After the installation of new floodlights at Anfield in 1970 Ray Clemence had to obtain a large peaked cap to stop his eyes being dazzled.

With the prospect of moving to a new 100,000 all-seater stadium at Aintree now no longer on the horizon, ground improvements continued at Anfield in the close season. New floodlights were installed, and, as with everything at Anfield, to Shankly they were the greatest floodlights in the history of the game: 'Wonderful lights! wonderful lights!' he jubilantly told the local press. 'This is the first time you could really say this ground has been lit up … The effect on the players will be good under these new lights. It will be like coming out on to the pitch on a bright, sunny day. The players are bound to get some sort of boost.'

Above: Arsenal players assist Liverpool's Chris Lawler during the 1971 F A Cup final.

Left: Kevin Keegan sits on a dustbin outside Anfield waiting for Bill Shankly to arrive to sign him up in 1971.

Shankly's players were gathered round listening to their manager talking about the extra power of the new floodlights, and the new first-team goal-keeper, Ray Clemence, decided there and then that a new cap was needed with a large peak on it. On another occasion, Shankly told an incredulous press, 'Just look at that grass, boys. It's great grass at Anfield, professional grass.'

On the playing front, at the start of the 1970-71 season, with only four wins out of their first eleven games, the new floodlights clearly hadn't give the Liverpool team the type of boost Shankly had anticipated. But the dashing winger Steve Heighway, who had been signed for nothing from a local amateur team Skelmersdale, would soon be introduced to the team along with John Toshack. Toshack cost Liverpool a £110,000 fee from Cardiff City, but the tall Welshman, along with Heighway, would prove to be an outstanding acquisition to the team.

Although Liverpool were never really in contention in the League, Shankly's blossoming new team put together a good run in the F A Cup. Their opponents in the semi-final were Everton. Goals from Evans and Hall in a tense encounter gave Liverpool a 2-1 victory. They were through to Wembley for the first time since 1965, their opponents Arsenal.

Prior to the final, Shankly signed a player who had been strongly recommended to him by his former team-mate at Preston, Andy Beattie, who had spotted Kevin Keegan playing for Scunthorpe and was immediately impressed by this darting, irrepressible youngster, who played his heart out for the full 90 minutes. Shankly got Keegan for £35,000, a sum later described by the Liverpool boss as 'robbery with violence', and the son of a Yorkshire miner would go on to become one of the all-time Liverpool greats. With Ray Clemence also being snapped up from Scunthorpe, and later Keegan, both of whom would go on to become

Shankly hides his disappointment after defeat against Arsenal in the 1971 F A Cup final

world-class performers, it can't be emphasised enough just what a key role the lowly Yorkshire club played in the construction of Shankly's second great team.

* * *

With Liverpool back at Wembley, the demand for tickets was as intense as ever. Shankly did his best to try and supply as many genuine Liverpool supporters as he could, but it was always a losing battle. On the day of the game, Liverpool, who had won the toss to play in their normal red strip, took to the field confident they could stop Arsenal completing the League and Cup double for only the second time this century. Liverpool took the lead through Heighway, but struggled to dominate the game. Shankly had said beforehand, 'We've got to Wembley with a team of boys that will last for ten years.' With Keegan now in the squad, though unavailable for the final, Shankly did have a squad who would go on to dominate the game throughout the 1970s. But against Arsenal their time hadn't yet come.

F A CUP SEMI-FINAL
27 March 1971

Liverpool	2
Everton	1

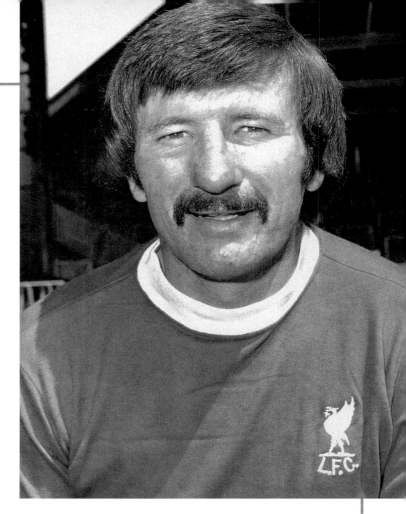

The F A Cup semi-final of 1971 between Liverpool and Everton is widely regarded as one of the greatest Merseyside derby games of the century. Hopes were high that this might finally be the year when the two football giants would meet each other at Wembley for the first time, but the draw pitted them together. Everton were reigning League Champions, with England players of the calibre of Wright, Newton, Labone and Ball in their team. Shankly was still developing his second great team, so Evertonians were confident that a place at Wembley would be forthcoming.

'In 1971, we were still trying to guess just how good the "new" Liverpool team might be and, frankly, I was a little worried about nerves on the part of our players, for several of them were still learning what it was all about,' recalled Bob Paisley.

With the outstanding midfield line-up of Ball, Harvey and Kendall in full flow, Everton took a first-half lead when Ray Clemence misjudged a Morrissey cross and Ball slotted in the opener. Everton went in at the interval 1-0 in the lead. Shankly got to work on his team, telling them, 'You're playing too many high balls. You need a ladder to get to them.'

With just four minutes gone in the second half, Everton's centre-half, Brian Labone, suffered a hamstring injury and had to go off. Sandy Brown replaced Labone in the Everton defence, but didn't have the commanding presence of the England international. After Labone's departure, Liverpool took the initiative and a Heighway cross found Alun Evans who shot past Andy Rankin in the Everton goal. Everton's heads dropped and Liverpool were now pressing for a winner.

Their second came from Brian Hall, playing his first team game at Old Trafford. Evans sent over a cross and after some scrimmaging in the penalty area, the ball fell to Hall, who hooked the ball into the net: 'I'd scored my first goal for Liverpool – the winning goal in a semi-final – against

Everton! When you put it all together, it added up to something that will stay with me for ever.'

Tommy Smith was man-of-the-match and Shankly declared after the game, 'If Tommy Smith isn't named Footballer of the Year, then football should be stopped and the men who pick any other player should be sent to the Kremlin.'

Everton's manager Harry Catterick missed the game through illness and when Shankly heard about this, he exclaimed, 'Sickness wouldn't have kept me away from this one. If I'd been dead, I would have had them bring the casket to the ground, pop it up in the stands and cut a hole in the lid.'

Liverpool: Clemence, Lawler, Lindsay, Smith, Lloyd, Hughes, Callaghan, Evans, Heighway, Toshack, Hall

Everton: Rankin, T Wright, K Newton, Kendall, Labone (Brown, 49 min), Harvey, Whittle, Ball, Royle, Hurst, Morrisey

Arsenal equalised Heighway's effort and went on to win the game through an outstanding Charlie George effort. 'The long-haired George may look like someone who has strayed in from the nearest discotheque, but this boy is a great player,' said one paper. If Shankly had snapped up Keegan a few months earlier, the player who would go on to galvanise what was obviously a talented team although still lacking penetration, may have given Liverpool that extra something that was needed to defeat a well-organised Arsenal. Tommy Smith recently recalled that he was so disappointed after the 1971 final that he was violently ill after

trudging back to the dressing room. 'I can still remember Charlie George lying on the ground with that smug look on his face after he had scored that crucial goal,' Smith lamented.

The following day, Liverpool were welcomed back to Liverpool by over 100,000 disappointed fans. Brian Hall remembers that the Liverpool manager was locked deep in thought as he waved to the fans from an open-topped bus. Shankly turned to the young Liverpool player and demanded, 'Hey son, who's that Chinaman, you know the one with the sayings? What's his name?' The university-educated Hall thought, 'Are you

Bill Shankly and his backroom staff try to revitalise tired Liverpool limbs before the period of extra time in the 1971 F A Cup final.

barmy, or what?' Hall told Shankly, 'Is it Chairman Mao you mean?' 'That's him, son,' replied an excited Shankly. Hall forgot about Shankly's bizarre question until the team arrived at St George's Hall. As thousands flocked around the Victorian building, Shankly came to the microphone and began to speak: 'Ladies and gentlemen, yesterday at Wembley, we may have lost the Cup, but you the people have won everything. You have won over the policemen in London. You won over the London public, and it's questionable if Chairman Mao of China could have arranged such a show of strength as you have shown yesterday and today.' The multitudes roared their approval.

Shankly had the ability to lift his team if they lost, and now he made the Liverpool supporters feel on top of the world after a disappointing Wembley defeat. Shankly knew that something special was needed and came up with the perfect uplifting speech. Brian Hall shook his head and recalls thinking 'This man's a genius'.

* * *

When Shankly gathered his squad together for the start of the pre-season training, before the 1971-72 season, they were both surprised and amused at the new arrival Kevin Keegan. The fanatically keen newcomer wanted to be first in everything. 'I had to simmer him down,' recalled Shankly. '"You don't train like that, son," I told him. He wanted to win every race in training. I had to tell him to take it easy, you're only preparing to train.'

Tommy Smith and the other experienced Liverpool first-teamers nicknamed Keegan 'Kevin McDaft' but pretty soon they became as bowled over by Keegan as the training staff at Anfield were. Bob Paisley, remembering Keegan's arrival at Anfield, said, 'He had infectious enthusiasm, boundless stamina and seemed to love every kick of the game. Joe Fagan and I were impressed by the fact that he had a buzz about him every time he got the ball.'

It was originally planned that Keegan would take over the Ian Callaghan role, operating up and down the right-hand side of midfield; Callaghan was struggling after a cartilage operation. But as it turned out, the now fit again Callaghan reverted to

Bill Shankly before giving his famous Chairman Mao speech after Liverpool's 1971 F A Cup final defeat against Arsenal.

his midfield role and Keegan was an instant success playing up front with Toshack.

* * *

Liverpool opened the season with four wins in their first five games, and prospects looked good for a title-winning season. With double winners Arsenal competing in the European Cup, Liverpool were England's representatives in the European Cup Winners' Cup. They had the misfortune, however, to draw Bayern Munich in the second round and lost 3-1 on aggregate to the talented Germans.

Liverpool remained in contention though in the League until the final game of the season. An incredible end-of-season run, with thirteen wins in their last sixteen games, saw them come within a whisker of the title, but it was to be Brian Clough's Derby County who would be crowned as champions.

Ballet in the air at Anfield – John Toshack challenges Chelsea's David Webb and Gary Locke for the ball in 1972.

Liverpool's attack wasn't yet firing on all cylinders, but their defence was developing into the meanest in the League, conceding just 30 goals. Shankly's great team of the 1960s had been built on the 'Attack, Attack, Attack' principle; his next great team was built on a defence that gave nothing away, and exciting forwards like Keegan and Heighway who could create goals out of nothing.

During the early 1970s Shankly told an interviewer the type of team he was hoping to develop at Anfield: 'I want to build a team that's invincible, so that they have to send a team from bloody Mars to beat us.'

* * *

The Liverpool team that won the double of the League Championship and UEFA Cup in season 1972-73 could have been just the type of line-up he had in mind. Shankly brought in the excellent

ALEC LINDSAY

Alec Lindsay was signed from his home club, Bury, in 1969 for a £68,000 fee, and was tried in a variety of positions before settling down to the left-back spot.

Lindsay featured in a famous Shankly anecdote which told the tale of the full-back suffering pre-match nerves before his first-team debut. Shankly, noticing the state the player was in, put his arm on Lindsay's shoulder to give him some last-minute instructions, 'Alec, when you get the ball, I want you to beat a couple of players and smash the ball into the net, just the way you used to at Bury.' Alec Lindsay looked up at Shankly, scratched his head and muttered, 'But Boss, that wasn't me, it's Jimmy Kerr you're thinking of!' With that Shankly turned to Bob Paisley and exclaimed, 'Jesus Christ! Bob, we've only gone and signed the wrong bloody player!'

Lindsay eventually settled down into an outstanding full-back and four England caps followed. Probably his best seasons were the Championship-winning year of 1973, followed by the F A Cup-winning season of 1974. He never quite lived up to the high expectations that Liverpool had of him and he was transferred to Stoke in 1977. Lindsay played for Liverpool 244 times, scoring 18 goals.

Peter Cormack from Nottingham Forest for a £110,000 fee in the summer of 1972 to supplement the squad. The Anfield faithful looked forward to the new season with relish.

Shankly and his backroom staff had also developed a style of play that they hoped would minimise the risk of injury. Shankly recalled, 'The team played in sections of the field, like a relay. We didn't want players running the length of the field, stretching themselves unnecessarily, so our back men played in one area, and then passed on to the midfield men in their area, and so on to the front men. So, whilst there was always room for individuals within our system, the work was shared out.'

Four wins in their first five games gave Liverpool a great start to the season. The *Liverpool Echo* was in no doubt that this was going to be a successful season for the team, 'By now, the whole of the First Division will have got the message. It's quite clear – Liverpool are a team to fear this season.' A female

Left: An all-star gathering at Anfield for Roger Hunt's testimonial game in 1972. Over 56,000 attended the game in honour of the Anfield hero they called Sir Roger.

Below: Ian Callaghan scoring against Hull City in the 1973 F A Cup; he went on to get a hat-trick.

Koppite collated the songs and chants that were popular during this period and some were reproduced in an article she penned for a local paper. She wrote, 'I can't say I'm fond of the song in which they bawl "We only carry hatchets to bury in their 'eads". But the Kop are always quick to spot something new. To Tommy Smith when he trotted out for the first time in white boots, they sang "Where did you get those boots, where did you get those boots". "Toshack is the king" was sung to the tune of "Men of Harlech", and to Malcolm Macdonald during a recent Newcastle visit "Super Mac is only good when it's raining" to the tune of "Michael, Row the Boat Ashore"'.

The Kop were in good voice as Liverpool powered their way to their first title of the 1970s. They had never been content to just watch, they had to be an active part of the communal Anfield experience. They were certainly a part of the celebrations when Shankly and his team paraded around Anfield with the Championship trophy after a goalless draw against Leicester assured them of the title.

Bill Shankly's second great team are League Champions in 1973. 'I want to build a team that's invincible, so that they have to send a team from bloody Mars to beat us,' he said.

* * *

LARRY LLOYD

Bristol-born Larry Lloyd had played only one full season for Bristol Rovers when Liverpool stepped in and paid £60,000 for the giant centre-half. Shankly saw Lloyd as the natural replacement for Ron Yeats, who was nearing the end of his glittering Anfield career. Lloyd had first come to Liverpool's attention after they had witnessed how well he had handled Joe Royle in an F A Cup game at Goodison Park. They had also watched him prior to this game in a 2-1 Bristol Rovers victory at Tranmere that same season.

Lloyd took over the centre-half spot in season 1970-71 and it looked like a long Anfield career was on the cards for the tough-tackling giant of a player. He was bowled over by the confidence-building pre-match pep talks of Shankly and on one occasion recalled the Liverpool boss telling the team to take their shirts off and throw them to Ronnie Moran, 'We were playing Ipswich and he came rushing into the dressing room and said, "Right, sit back down. Take off your shirts." I thought, what the hell is going on here. Shankly then said to Ronnie Moran, "Throw those shirts out on to the park, because those shirts alone will beat this Ipswich team!" We were chomping at the bit then. We went out and beat them 4-2. You knew it was nonsense, but it was brilliant nonsense!'

Once again, as with so many players at the club, an injury sidelined Lloyd and he never regained his place. Phil Thompson took his position at the heart of the defence, alongside Emlyn Hughes, and never looked back. Though available, Lloyd wasn't chosen for the 1974 F A Cup final and decided to try his luck the following season at Coventry, the Midlands club paying £225,000 for his services.

In Europe too, Liverpool were only two games away from success in the UEFA Cup, after a hard-fought semi-final victory over Spurs. Liverpool's opponents in the final were Borussia Mönchengladbach. The first leg was due to be played at Anfield on the 9 May, but torrential rain meant that only 20 minutes' play was possible. John Toshack had been dropped for the abandoned game and had exchanged words with Shankly. The Welsh player, thinking that his days at Liverpool had probably come to a close, had driven home to tell his wife that he would be looking for a new club soon. Within minutes of arriving home, Shankly was on the phone telling him to prepare himself for that night's rearranged game; the Liverpool manager had spotted the previous night that the Germans had looked vulnerable to high crosses, and Toshack was just the man to exploit this. Brian Hall was the

unlucky player who had to make way for Toshack's return, 'I remember that evening vividly because I thought I'd be wearing the same number as the night before. Shanks didn't see it that way of course. He decided a tactical change was needed. At the end of the day, Shanks was right because we won 3-0. I'd have argued at the time that we would have won 4-0 if I'd played, but I think I'd be being a bit naive if I said that.'

In the return leg Borussia Mönchengladbach put Liverpool under severe pressure, but Liverpool held out to take the UEFA Cup 3-2 on aggregate. Shankly, at long last, had won his first European trophy. Although winning the UEFA Cup gave Shankly great pleasure, it was his third League Championship that pleased him the most: 'That was the greatest triumph of all of them. Winning the Championship early on was a novelty. This one was won with a new team. This was definitely the greatest moment that I had in Football.'

Shankly had built a team that would dominate the game for the rest of the 1970s.

* * *

An estimated 250,000 ecstatic Merseysiders lined the streets of Liverpool as they triumphantly paraded the two trophies through the city. Shankly, wearing a

Above: Bill Shankly and Ronnie Moran. Former Reds' star David Johnson once said of Moran, 'There was never any pleasing him. He was always bollocking people. It was always his voice bawling across Melwood. I hated him when I was there. In retrospect, he was good for us all and has done a fantastic job down the years. Every successful club needs someone like Ronnie.'

Right: European success at last. Bill Shankly holds the UEFA Cup after Liverpool's victory over Borussia Mönchengladbach in 1973.

bright-red shirt, had never looked happier. When the motorcade reached Liverpool's Picton Library, the team alighted from their bus and Shankly spoke to the thousands massed in front of the building: 'This is the greatest day of my career. If there is any doubt that you are the greatest fans in the world, this is the night to prove it. We have won for you and that's all we are interested in, winning for you. The reason we have won is because we believe and you believe, and it's faith and interest that have won us something. Thank God we are all here. You don't know how much we love you.' With that, Shankly led the fans in a spontaneous rendition of 'You'll Never Walk Alone', the anthem of Anfield.

A Liverpool fan, eighty-four-year-old Herbert Murphy, who had been following the team since 1904, was asked for his opinions of Shankly. He replied, 'Quite honestly, I can think of no man I admire more than him. I admire him for the same reason everyone admires him and that's for putting Liverpool where they are today and for being such a credit to the game.'

If Shankly had called it a day there and then, the jubilant Scot couldn't have ended on a happier note. But there was one more great success to come before the legend of Anfield bowed out. ●

Right: Kevin Keegan and Phil Thompson at Liverpool's triumphant homecoming with the 1973 Championship and UEFA Cup trophies.

Below: Liverpool boxer John Conteh displays his World Championship belt and Tommy Smith the UEFA Cup at Liverpool's homecoming reception in 1973.

THE UEFA CUP FINAL (first leg)
10 May 1973

Liverpool	**3**
Borussia Mönchengladbach	**0**

This was the European final that cost just 10p to attend. After the initial game was abandoned the previous evening due to a rainstorm, Liverpool decided to charge just a nominal entrance fee for the rearranged game. Bill Shankly had noticed in the 27 minutes' play of the initial game, before it was abandoned, that the German side were susceptible to high crosses into the penalty area, and decided that John Toshack, with his formidable heading ability, would cause Borussia a lot of problems. Shankly's hunch proved correct and Toshack's headwork was a key factor in Liverpool's success.

The Keegan/Toshack partnership was never seen to better effect than in the 21st minute when Toshack leapt above the Borussia defence to head a Lawler cross into the path of Keegan, who dived to head a sensational goal past Kleff. In the 33rd minute, Liverpool went two up when Toshack again connected with a Hughes pass to lay on goal number two for Keegan, who shot past the Borussia goalkeeper. Keegan had, in fact, missed the opportunity to put Liverpool two ahead five minutes earlier when he missed a penalty after a Borussia defender handled a Lindsay cross. The German keeper appeared to move well before Keegan hit the penalty kick and the shot was saved by the right post. Borussia should have scored themselves in the 29th minute when Danner had an easy opportunity, but he struck his shot against the post.

In the second half, Borussia pushed forward in a bid to score an important away goal. This gave Liverpool the chance to hit the Germans on the break. After a period of Liverpool pressure, centre-half Larry Lloyd found himself unmarked in the penalty area for a 62nd minute corner that he dispatched in the Borussia net. The German side refused to give in, and just two minutes later they won a penalty after Steve Heighway brought down Jensen in the penalty area. Heynckes blasted the kick to Clemence's right, but the Liverpool keeper pulled off an outstanding save, throwing himself to the ground to keep the ball out. Liverpool's defence, inspired by the outstanding Clemence, kept Borussia at bay until the end of the game. After nine seasons of trying, Liverpool's first European trophy was now in sight.

Interviewed after the game, Ray Clemence admitted that he had watched Heynckes take a penalty kick on television during Borussia's semi-final game, and decided to dive in the same direction that that shot was struck: 'The save was a reward for my homework,' said a delighted Clemence. Bill Shankly congratulated both teams for the magnificent display of football, but said the final was far from over: 'I don't make any predictions for the second leg. It's half time at the moment. The important thing is that we did not give a goal away. It was a fantastic performance by us. It was a high-class game – an international class game. Both teams did well and it wasn't a case of what Borussia did wrong, it was what we did right.'

Borussia coach, Hennes Wiesweiler, gave his team little chance in the second-leg. 'I think our chances of winning the trophy have disappeared. Liverpool are the best side we have played in the competition. They are very attractive, full of power and very strong. I can't say I fancy our chances now.'

Liverpool: Clemence, Lawler, Lindsay, Smith, Lloyd, Hughes, Keegan, Cormack, Toshack, Heighway (Hall, 84 min), Callaghan.

Borussia Mönchengladbach: Keiff, Danner, Michallich, Vogts, Benhof, Kulik, Jensen, Wimmer, Rupp, (Simmonson, 83 min), Netzer, Heynckes.

Kevin Keegan scores Liverpool's first goal in the 3-0 victory over Mönchengladbach.

CHAPTER NINE

1973-74

LIKE WALKING TO THE ELECTRIC CHAIR

The Shankly Years Come To An End

'I said to him, "How's your retirement, Boss?" He said, "Retirement! The man who invented the word should be shot!" Shanks was cast adrift from the game. He was always a leader and now he had nothing to lead.'

Ian St John, on Bill Shankly's retirement

Emlyn Hughes hold the F A Cup aloft after Liverpool's 1974 F A Cup victory against Newcastle.

Shankly's emerging young team began the 1973-74 season confident that they could emulate the achievements of Celtic and Manchester United, and bring the European Cup back to British shores. Their defence of the title didn't start too well, however, as they won only four of their first nine games.

In the first round of the European Cup they also made an unconvincing start, beating the part-timers of Luxembourg, Jeunesse D'Esch, just 3-1 over the two legs. They were matched against Red Star Belgrade in the next round. Red Star were a useful team, but if Liverpool had played with anything like the same fervour that had swept them to the Championship the previous season, they would have won the tie. As it turned out, Red Star brought to an end Shankly's last crack at the

European Cup before it had had a chance to build up momentum, winning the tie 4-2 on aggregate.

Liverpool, and in particular heir apparent to the manager's chair, Bob Paisley, would gain from the Red Star defeat and learn how to sit back and then hit teams on the break with devastating results. In European competition, patience was most definitely a virtue. Shankly's style of play was based on tactics and passion, and he once described himself as 'an impatient, patient man'. To win at the highest level in Europe, the European Cup, a tactician was needed whose patient elements of his nature heavily outweighed the impatient parts. Shankly undoubtedly laid the foundations for Liverpool's incredible success in Europe over the next decade; a Geordie, with a deep understanding of the game, Bob Paisley would build on the foundations that Shankly had laid.

* * *

With the dream of success in the European Cup gone, Liverpool turned their attention back to domestic competition. They regained their consistency and pushed Leeds all the way for the Championship, but the outstanding Yorkshire team couldn't be overtaken and took the title by five points.

Chelsea's Ray Wilkins tackles Kevin Keegan during a 1970s Anfield encounter.

It was in the F A Cup that Shankly's team, after some early round scares, really excelled. They put out Doncaster, but only after a hard-fought replay in the third round, and were then drawn against Carlisle. The first game at Anfield resulted in a 0-0 draw. Liverpool travelled to Brunton Park expecting a difficult time, but their class came to their aid and they won comfortably 2-0. After the game, the Carlisle manager Alan Ashman was asked his opinions on Shankly's Liverpool. He told the press, 'Liverpool are wholehearted. They fit into the Shankly style of play; which is all action. Liverpool and Leeds have been the top two teams over the past ten years. The yardstick of a good side is how

they have been playing for years. It amazes me how Liverpool keep it going. I can't see them ever being anything less than a good side. I hope they go on and win the F A Cup.'

In the next rounds, Liverpool defeated Ipswich, Bristol City and Leicester to get to Wembley where their opponents would be Newcastle United, who were as desperate, if not more so, for success. Newcastle hadn't won a domestic trophy since the early 1950s, when they won the F A Cup three years out of five. A classic final was anticipated, particularly when Newcastle's Malcolm Macdonald made it known that he would make sure that the Liverpool defence had a difficult afternoon; he was

Peter Cormack in action against Arsenal during Liverpool's triumphant title-winning season of 1972-73.

F A CUP SEMI-FINAL REPLAY
3 April 1974

Leicester	1
Liverpool	3

Liverpool's Kevin Keegan gave probably his greatest display yet in a red shirt with a goal that had the press searching for superlatives adequate enough to describe it. With both teams committed to attack from start to finish, the game was rightly described as a classic. The match began at a terrific pace with England's top two goalkeepers, Ray Clemence and Peter Shilton, needing to be at their best to keep the score level at half-time.

Just 35 seconds after the break, Liverpool took the lead. After a goalmouth scramble, Leicester's Keith Weller and Brian Hall of Liverpool both fought for the ball on the line. Hall managed to knock the ball into the net and Liverpool were in front.

Within three minutes, Leicester were back on level terms, Earle and Stringfellow having burst through the Liverpool defence, and when Earle shot the ball, it glanced off a Liverpool defender into the path of Glover who shot into an empty Liverpool goal. Clemence then had to produce a magnificent save from Weller to stop Leicester taking the lead. It was end-to-end stuff with Liverpool and Leicester throwing caution to the wind. The Leicester defence didn't appear to be in any danger when Toshack lobbed a ball forward in the 61st minute, until Keegan came running in at speed to outstrip the Leicester defenders and volley the ball past Shilton from 20 yards out.

Keegan's wonder goal knocked the heart out of Leicester and 4 minutes from the end, Cormack split the Leicester defence with an inch perfect pass to Toshack, who strode into the penalty area before coolly shooting past Shilton. Liverpool had booked their place at Wembley.

The dejected Leicester team walked off the pitch with their heads slumped, but they had contributed hugely to one of the most exciting F A Cup semi-finals of the post-war years. They were just unfortunate to come up against a Liverpool team who were on top form. Leicester manager, Jimmy Bloomfield, said after the match, 'It was a very tight match, but in the end, they were the better side. When we got the equaliser, I thought we were really in with a chance. We're bitterly disappointed.'

The Liverpool camp were overjoyed at getting to Wembley again. Phil Thompson, who played the game with his wrist in a plaster, said he was looking forward to meeting Newcastle in the final, and in particular Malcolm Macdonald: 'The game was played at 100 miles an hour – or so it seemed – now we can silence Malcolm Macdonald at Wembley.' Kevin Keegan, scorer of the goal of the season, remarked, 'I've done it a million times in training but never in a match. I've constantly practised these flicks on the volley and this time, I just happened to get it right. We proved we can outlast other teams in matches like this, which are so tense.'

Bill Shankly was overjoyed to get to the F A Cup final in what he, but nobody else, knew would be his last season at Liverpool. He said, 'This was a magnificent match. Both teams were a credit. We played as well as we have ever played. We played class football from the back, moving the ball around with skill and flair. It was marvellous to watch in such an electric atmosphere.' He added that all of his team showed 'collective brilliance', but singled out Smith, Callaghan, Hall and Cormack for special praise. As for Kevin Keegan, Shankly remarked, 'He has scored many brilliant goals this season, but this was his most important. That was the killer goal for Leicester. All round he gave a fantastic display. But what is unbelievable to me is that he isn't in the England side. It's nothing short of criminal. In fact, it's like hanging an innocent man!'

Leicester: Shilton, Whitworth, Rofe, Earle, Munroe, Cross, Weller, Sammels, Worthington, Stringfellow, Glover. Sub, Waters

Liverpool: Clemence, Smith, Lindsay, Thompson, Cormack, Hughes, Keegan, Hall, Heighway, Toshack, Callaghan. Sub, Boersma

Kevin Keegan celebrates his stunning goal against Leicester.

undoubtedly a formidable player and had once scored a hat-trick against Liverpool. Tommy Smith had sidled up to Macdonald after that game and told him in no uncertain terms that he'd scored his last goal against Liverpool. Smith reminded Macdonald of this as the two teams lined up in the Wembley tunnel before the game, and whether this played on Macdonald's mind is unknown, but 'Supermac', as he was known to the Newcastle fans who idolised him, was virtually anonymous throughout the final. Smith, in fact, left Macdonald to Phil Thompson, who had an outstanding game and kept such a firm grip on Macdonald that Tommy Smith spent much of the game foraging up the right wing setting up goal-scoring opportunities.

Liverpool's emphatic 3-0 victory demonstrated everything that Shankly held dear. Their passing was crisp and precise and up front, they had flair and a cutting edge. Goals from Steve Heighway, and two from Kevin Keegan gave Liverpool a comfortable victory, in one of the most one-sided finals seen at Wembley.

After the game, Prime Minister Harold Wilson, who was a genuine football fan and rarely missed a Wembley final, remarked, 'I said before the game that once Keegan and Heighway start moving then the result won't be in doubt. I forecast 2-1 to Liverpool before the match. If it had gone on for another ten minutes it might have been 5-0.' The only crumb of comfort for two of the outclassed Newcastle team, McDermott and Kennedy, was that soon they would be joining Liverpool and become a part of the successful Anfield scene themselves.

Shankly declined the opportunity to go on his team's lap of honour, and instead stood quietly taking in the euphoria. Several Liverpool fans ignored the team and went up to Shankly and kissed his feet, a spontaneous act of homage to their messiah. There can be little doubt that the Anfield faithful held their team in the highest esteem. But their ultimate acclamation was for a sixty-year-old Scot, a man they worshipped.

Interviewed after the game, as he sat quietly tucking into a celebratory pork pie and mug of tea,

Kevin Keegan and Ian Callaghan parade the F A Cup around Wembley in 1974.

Shankly said, 'I'm happy, not for me, no. I'm happy for the players, training staff, directors, but above all I'm happy for the multitudes. I'm a people's man, I'm a socialist and I'm happy for them because I work for them. I'm just sorry that I couldn't go in among them and speak to all of them. The people who came on to the field and bowed down to me. These are the people I'm pleased for more than anybody else.'

Turning to his team, Shankly knew that he had a squad who could win trophies for several more years. 'The great team of the 1960s won the League in 1964, the Cup in 1965 and the League again in 1966. Without doubt, this is the best team in the League, they can go on to do the same as the 1960s team.'

* * *

Liverpool arrived back on Merseyside to the greatest

STEVE HEIGHWAY

Dublin-born Steve Heighway was recommended to Liverpool by Bob Paisley's sons, who had spotted him playing amateur football for Skelmersdale. Paisley decided to take a look for himself and had no doubts about telling Bill Shankly to sign him.

Heighway, a dashing winger with electric pace, was a revelation when introduced into the team. There was also the added bonus of his ability to regularly get himself on the score sheet. Heighway made 444 appearances for Liverpool, scoring 76 goals in the process, which was a high ratio for a player who was predominantly a winger. His growing prowess also brought him to the attention of the Eire selectors and he was awarded 34 international caps.

Much of the success of the Keegan/Toshack partnership can be put down to the wing play of Heighway, who set up many of their goal-scoring opportunities. 'Heighway, can win a match with one flash of genius,' Shankly once remarked.

Steve Heighway left Liverpool to try his luck in America in 1981 with Minnesota Kicks, but today he is back at Anfield helping to produce the stars of the future.

homecoming they had ever received. An estimated 500,000 lined the streets to welcome home Shankly's Wembley heroes. The *Liverpool Daily Post* agreed with Shankly's sentiments that this team had the potential to become the greatest in the club's history, saying, 'Not even this 3-0 hammering paid adequate tribute to the overwhelming might, majesty and ascendancy of Liverpool in a football fantasy that made a Newcastle nightmare in broad daylight. It was a victory which must have ended all those comparisons with the great side of the 1960s. This side can become the greatest of them all. In fourteen years with Bill Shankly, Liverpool have learned to walk with pride. They have never known a finer hour than this.'

Once again, Shankly spoke to the mass of supporters, who listened intently to his every word. 'I think today, I feel prouder than I have ever done

continued on page 127

THE F A CUP FINAL
4 May 1974

Liverpool	**3**
Newcastle	**0**

The F A Cup final of 1974 was one of the most eagerly awaited finals in years. Liverpool and Leeds were undoubtedly the two best teams in the country at that time, but Newcastle were packed with outstanding individuals as well. The outspoken Malcolm Macdonald certainly added extra spice to the occasion by telling anyone who would listen that the Merseyside club were in for a torrid afternoon, but he wasn't all mouth, as given the chance he could dispatch the ball into the net with consummate ease. His partner up-front, John Tudor, was also a clinical goalscorer. Newcastle also had the promising Terry McDermott and Alan Kennedy, later to join the Reds, in their line-up. With the potentially brilliant Terry Hibbitt prompting them from mid-field, it was with some justification that they fancied their chances.

Bill Shankly once said, 'When I go to see a team I want to see a system. I watch some teams and don't know what the hell they are trying to do. Some teams play like total strangers. In other words, they're not on speaking terms. At Liverpool, the method is preparation and adjustment. When a Liverpool player gets the ball, his mate knows where to go. They all know each other.'

Liverpool's display against Newcastle personified everything Shankly was looking for in his team. The beaten Newcastle team were the team who played like 'total strangers' on this occasion.

The first half was a half of sparring, with Liverpool slightly better team. After the interval, Liverpool were magnificent, with each of their team totally on top of their game. 'Every one of my players were stars' was Shankly's comment after the game.

Keegan opened the scoring after 58 minutes,

brilliantly volleying home a Smith cross. In the 75th minute Heighway scored from a Toshack header. Liverpool were now rampant and Keegan scored again from a Smith centre in the 88th minute to confirm Liverpool's superiority. It was one of the greatest 45 minutes of play put on by a team at Wembley this century, and Newcastle couldn't live with it. After the game, Terry McDermott, a Kirkby lad through and through, was dejected, but achieved one of his greatest ambitions, which was to wear the red shirt of Liverpool. McDermott exchanged his Newcastle top with Liverpool's Kirkby youngster, Phil Thompson. Within a few months McDermott would be joining Thompson in the Liverpool team on his way to many Liverpool trophy-winning glories of his own.

A delighted Shankly told the press afterwards, 'A lot of people in the press were making predictions about the final. They were analysing our team and hadn't even seen us play. This annoyed me. It's like trying to analyse [champion boxer] Jack Dempsey without seeing him bloody fighting.'

Two-goal hero Kevin Keegan said, 'I'll never play in a game with that much atmosphere for the rest of my life. Not even a World Cup final.' He was to reveal in later years how Bill Shankly psyched up his team before the game began: 'He pinned up on the notice board an article that Malcolm Macdonald had done. Shanks said, "There you are, boys, that's what they're going to do to us." We all read it and it said all the things you shouldn't say before a match; we had no pace, we were overrated. When we went out, we just wanted to make him eat his words, and we did.'

Liverpool: Clemence, Smith, Lindsay, Thompson, Cormack, Hughes, Keegan, Hall, Heighway, Toshack, Callaghan. Substitute, Lawler

Newcastle United: McFaul, Clark, Kennedy, McDermott, Howard, Moncur, Cassidy, Smith (Gibb), Macdonald, Tudor, Hibbitt

Ian Callaghan, surrounded by Newcastle defenders
Kennedy, Howard and McDermott in the 1974 F A Cup final.

KEVIN KEEGAN

'Kevin Keegan is one of the greatest players of all time. His exploits will never be forgotten. It makes you proud to know him. He went into the unknown and did it himself' – that was Bill Shankly talking about one of the Liverpool all-time greats.

Keegan was brought to the club initially to replace Ian Callaghan, playing wide on the right. Callaghan was struggling for fitness after a cartilage operation, but eventually forced his way back into the team. Shankly decided to try Keegan as a striker, and on his debut against Nottingham Forest in 1971, he scored after just 7 minutes.

His all-action approach created danger out of nothing and there was excitement and anticipation every time he got the ball; he was a hard player to keep a hold on, as many First Division defenders would soon find out.

England honours quickly came his way and in no time at all Keegan was being acclaimed as English football's new superstar. Ironically, he nearly missed out on one of the greatest moments; his two-goal performance in Liverpool's emphatic 3-0 victory in the 1974 F A Cup final against Newcastle, after being on the receiving end of a crunching tackle in a pre-match training session by none other that Bill Shankly himself. Fortunately, Keegan's injury cleared up in time for him to make the final.

After 331 appearances, and 100 goals, Keegan left Liverpool for £500,000 to join S V Hamburg. Although only at Liverpool for six seasons, Keegan won 3 Championship medals, 2 UEFA Cup winners' medals, a European Cup winners' medal and an F A Cup winners' medal. The dynamic Kevin Keegan will be remembered at Anfield for eternity.

continued from page 123

before. I said three years ago we would go back to Wembley. Not only did the team win the Cup yesterday, they gave an exhibition of football. But above all, we are pleased for you. It's you we play for. It's you who pay our wages. Not only did we win the Cup on the field, but we won it on the terraces as well.'

His final speech to the multitudes once again was greeted with rapturous applause. As the youngest member of the Liverpool team looked around him at the massive crowds that packed the city centre, he found it hard to believe that he was now an established member of the team he had supported from the terraces as a boy; Phil

Thompson recalled, 'I remember in 1965, we were all standing on top of a car watching the team return with the F A Cup. I'm one of the Kop really. I don't know what I'm doing playing for the team. I want to be with the Kop half the time.' Shankly knew exactly what the Liverpool youngster was doing in the team, but the sentiments expressed by Thompson could have come from the Liverpool boss himself.

* * *

With the F A Cup in the Anfield trophy cabinet, and an outstanding young team who looked destined for further success, Liverpool supporters looked set to enjoy the summer break safe in the knowledge that all was well at Anfield.

Liverpool's triumphant homecoming after winning the 1974 F A Cup.

A Liverpool street party celebrating the 1974 F A Cup victory.

on to become one of the greatest midfielders who ever put on a Liverpool shirt.

When the news sank in that Shankly was leaving the club, there was a widespread feeling of disbelief. When asked years later how he felt on that fateful day, Shankly replied, 'It was the most difficult thing in the world, when I went to tell the chairman. It was like walking to the electric chair. That's the way I felt.'

He revealed in his autobiography that he had been thinking about it for over a year. He had always spent an incredible amount of time away from home, checking on players and opponents, or being the guest of honour at some social function. Shankly always gave 100 per cent effort to whatever task he set himself and he was mentally tired.

His wife Nessie said it was for her that he brought his football management career to a close, 'Last year I asked him to think about retirement and it's for me he has announced it. Bill's as fit as a fiddle, but you can be fit and still be tired. He gives so much of himself to the game.'

continued on page 132

Above: Bill Shankly with the F A Cup in 1974.

Right: Peter Robinson, club secretary during the Shankly era and later the club's chief executive. He tried hard to keep Shankly at Liverpool.

A surprise press conference was called at the club on 12 July as many were either at work or away on a summer break; mass unemployment having not yet hit Merseyside on the scale it would after the 1979 General Election.

When the news hit the airwaves that Bill Shankly had decided to retire, it was met with widespread disbelief. An Evertonian wind-up was the general consensus of those who hadn't yet had it confirmed on their radio sets or television screens. 'Why?' was the question on everyone's lips. 'He's not ill is he?' The other announcement that day by the Liverpool board, that they had just purchased Ray Kennedy from Arsenal for £200,000, didn't really concern them, though, as it turned out, Kennedy would go

THE F A CHARITY SHIELD
10 August 1974

Leeds	**1**
Liverpool	**1**

(Liverpool won on penalties)

The first Charity Shield game to be played at Wembley is also remembered as one of the most violent encounters to take place there.

Bill Shankly led Liverpool out onto the Wembley turf for the final time before handing over the managerial reins to Bob Paisley. Leeds also had a new manager, Brian Clough, who was taking over from Leeds legend Don Revie.

Shankly received a fantastic reception from both sets of supporters when he stepped out alone to lead the two teams out. Brian Clough then joined Shankly and applauded the Liverpool icon all the way to the halfway line. The scene was set for a showpiece game to start the new season. Champions Leeds, and Cup winners Liverpool were widely regarded as two of the best teams that English football had produced since the war.

Leeds against Liverpool games had always been physical encounters, but had never erupted into all-out war. Today was the day when this changed. The bad blood between the two teams manifested itself as early as the 10th minute.

'I played a pass forward and Allan Clarke, the Leeds striker, left his foot over the ball,' recalled Liverpool's Phil Thompson. 'The result was that my skin was ripped from my ankle up to my knee. The challenge incensed not only me but the whole Liverpool team. And it wasn't long before my old pal, Tommy Smith, got my revenge for me by up-ending Clarke. That match was later known for the incident in which Keegan and Bremner were both sent off. But it was Clarke who really started everything off in those first few minutes.'

Tommy Smith – who once said of Clarke, 'On the pitch, he's like an arsonist – he sparks off the blaze then retires to a safe distance to watch the fire' – was booked for scything down Clarke. The two teams then settled down to display the excellent football they were capable of. Phil Boersma

gave Liverpool a deserved lead and the game reached half-time without further incident.

Leeds came back at Liverpool after the break, but the game erupted in the 60th minute when Kevin Keegan and Billy Bremner were sent off for exchanging punches. The incident was initiated by Johnny Giles a few minutes earlier when he turned and punched Keegan, who was clipping at Giles's heels for the ball. Giles was booked for this offence. Referee Bob Matthewson was obviously reluctant to become the first official to send off a player from a British club at Wembley. A few minutes later, he was left with no options when Keegan and Bremner became embroiled in an unsavoury brawl. Both players then further exacerbated the situation by petulantly taking off their shirts and throwing them down on to the Wembley turf as they left the pitch.

Cherry was later to equalise for Leeds, before Liverpool took the Charity Shield on penalties, but the game would be remembered for the incidents that became newspaper headlines for many weeks to come. Both Keegan and Bremner had a hefty fine and a lengthy ban from the game imposed on them in the aftermath of their Wembley bust-up.

The incident that was described by one scribe as 'Wembley's Day of Shame' was even discussed in Parliament as violence on the field of play became a national issue. The *Daily Express* laid the blame for the incidents mainly on the shoulder of departing managers Bill Shankly and Don Revie, saying, 'Shankly and Revie have left behind not only exceptional football teams but several players who have been encouraged to believe they are entitled to exact their own kind of physical "justice" if they disagree with the referee or are beaten fair and square.'

After the game, Bill Shankly implied that the referee had overreacted in sending off Keegan and Bremner. To him, the game was nothing more than the usual red-blooded encounter between the two teams that had become commonplace over the years. He declined to comment on the sendings off but did buttonhole Billy Bremner in the dressing room to ask him why he threw his shirt on to the pitch. Bremner replied, 'I was just a bit disgusted with myself for getting involved.' Shankly

Brian Clough applauds Bill Shankly as they lead out Leeds and Liverpool for the 1974 Charity Shield.

answered, 'Aye, so you were. Now did you see that picture taken at a dinner the other week of yourself and me with [champion boxer] Jack Dempsey? Well, that man really could lick the world. It would have been the toughest half-back line of all time.'

Leeds: Harvey, Reaney, Cherry, Bremner, McQueen, Hunter, Lorimer, Clark (McKenzie, 59 min), Jordan, Giles, Gray (E)

Liverpool: Clemence, Smith, Lindsay, Thompson (P), Cormack, Hughes, Keegan, Hall, Heighway, Boersma, Callaghan

continued from page 129

Bill Shankly retires on 12 July 1974. 'It was the most difficult thing in the world when I went to tell the chairman. It was like walking to the electric chair. That's the way I felt,' explained Shankly.

It wasn't just the pressure of football that was taking its toll on Shankly, but some of the activities that he often gave himself willingly to that the media knew little of. 'Bill would often make visits to the local children's hospital at Alder Hey,' said Nessie. 'Some of the children were terminally ill and when he arrived home in the evening after visiting them he would break down in tears. It was because he didn't have the ability to make them better. I did suggest to him that perhaps he should think about taking a break from his hospital visits, and he would get angry and say, "I've said I'll visit the children and I'll go on visiting them," and that was that.'

Peter Robinson was Liverpool's club secretary at the time, and had built up a close working relationship with Shankly. Robinson, who is now the club's chief executive, revealed that he had spent the summer trying to get Shankly to change his mind, but once his decision was made, there was no going back. 'The board were desperate for him to stay in any capacity,' remembers Robinson. 'He could have any job he wanted. He said he was tired and needed a rest, so we said he could come in just one day a week if he wanted. But Bill was adamant and if I couldn't persuade him no one else could.'

Former Liverpool manager Joe Fagan, who worked with Shankly from day one of his arrival in 1959, has recently said that neither himself nor Bob Paisley, who were Shankly's two closest members of the backroom staff at the club, ever found out why he wanted to go.

* * *

Although he had retired from professional football, Shankly could still not get enough of the game and he kept up his daily training schedule, often at Liverpool's training ground at Melwood. The fans continued to worship the former Liverpool boss and if he was spotted at Anfield the chant would go up 'Shankly, Shankly, Shankly'. If he was at Goodison Park, the home of arch-rivals Everton, he would even get an ovation there. It was the same if he attempted to go shopping with Nessie into Liverpool city centre. Nessie recalls, 'Bill refused to walk past anyone if they stopped to say hello to him. He would stop and chat. When we went on shopping expeditions to Liverpool, we would always return empty-handed because Bill had spent the entire afternoon chatting to people. In the end we had to go to Manchester to do the shopping.'

Sunday afternoon was still the highlight of the week for Shankly. He would play in a match organised by local dads with their children. Dressed in his Liverpool tracksuit, it was the F A Cup final at Wembley all over again to Shankly, as he put every ounce of effort into making sure his side won.

* * *

Inevitably Shankly's training sessions at Melwood did lead to a certain amount of angst. The older professionals in the Liverpool squad found it hard to get out of the habit of referring to Shankly as 'Boss' and the new manager, Bob Paisley, was to them still 'Bob'. Liverpool wanted Paisley to be quickly accepted by the squad as the new manager and friction between the club and Shankly did develop. Shankly felt he was unwanted and took to watching the club's home games from different sections of the ground, rather than the directors' box. He even took up a fan's suggestion that he should come into the Kop.

Recalling this occasion, Shankly said, 'I went into the Kop, not out of bravado, but because I was their man. Not only the Kop, the Anfield Road, the Paddock, the Kemlyn Road, the whole of Anfield.' Once news spread that Shankly was in amongst them, the chant went up 'Shankly is our king, Shankly is our king' from a jubilant Kop.

Shankly continued to support his beloved Liverpool, but there was now a distance between himself and the club. He was in Rome for Liverpool's historic first European Cup victory in 1977, and when asked was he envious of Paisley's success, he replied, 'Too bloody right I am.'

* * *

It seemed to everyone that the superfit Shankly was incapable of even suffering a day's illness. He had always joked, 'When I die, I want people to walk past the coffin and say, "Christ, there lies a fit man!"' There was, therefore, a feeling of widespread disbelief throughout the football world when the news was relayed that Shankly had suffered a heart attack.

Bill Shankly displays the Charity Shield after the violent Leeds v. Liverpool game in 1974.

'Shankly is our king.'
Anfield salutes their hero
in 1975

He was rushed to hospital and it was thought that he was over the worst when a few days later his condition deteriorated again.

Bill Shankly died on 29 September 1981.

The staff and players of Liverpool Football Club, past and present, were heartbroken. Tommy Smith had had his run-ins with the man he now refers to as 'a soccer God' over the years, but, along with most of the Liverpool players from the Shankly era, thought the world of the man.

Bill Shankly had friends everywhere, not just those who were involved in the game, but the thousands he had shown kindness and encouragement to throughout the years. Today, eighteen years after his death, he remains a football icon.

In death, as in life, the spirit of Shankly dominates Liverpool Football Club. To a great many people on Merseyside and elsewhere, Shankly is the only real hero they will ever have in their lives. A smile inevitably comes to their faces, and a tear to their eyes, when former players and Liverpool fans talk about Shankly. To the many thousands who support the club, from near and afar, they are just grateful that they were around during the Shankly years.

*'My idea was to build Liverpool Football
club into a bastion of invincibility.
Napoleon had that idea. That's what I
wanted. Liverpool would be untouchable.
Up and up and up until eventually
everyone would have to submit.'*
Bill Shankly

CHAPTER TEN

THE SHANKLY LEGEND
He Made The
People Happy

'I was there when the Boss said that. It's been misquoted forever by people. Somebody was saying something to him about football being serious – "it's a matter of life or death". Shanks just gave the quip, "Nah, it's more serious than that," as a joke. He wasn't talking in depth about anything. It was just a quip. Everybody laughed. It wasn't said in the context that people think, believe me.'

Ian St John, on the famous Shankly 'life or death' quote

Kevin Keegan was recently quoted as saying, 'Liverpool should be playing in the Shankly Stadium now. There shouldn't just be a set of gates named after him.'

As we reach the year 2000, the Shankly legend grows stronger, not just with the Liverpool supporters past and present, but with his former players as well. Shankly's quips and post-match remarks are now repeated on a daily basis, and are even used to form questions on the 'who said this' section of television programmes such as *University Challenge*. No other football manager, past or present, is quite regarded in such esteem. Other managers have won numerous trophies, such as the great Sir Matt Busby at Manchester United and Shankly's magnificent successor at Liverpool, Bob Paisley. Both were also highly crucial figures, like Shankly, in building up their respective clubs into the world-famous empires they are today. But when was the last time you heard them quoted, or saw their former players

The great Bob Paisley embraces Bill Shankly before his 1975 benefit match. Paisley was a key and influential figure during the Shankly revolution at Anfield, and took over the managerial reins in sensational style.

close to tears when recounting some anecdote about them? The Shankly legend, and the stories about him, will continue to be told and retold because the man was unique.

Writing in 1980 when his former manager was still alive, Tommy Smith, who probably had more bust-ups with Shankly than any other Liverpool player, said, 'I still say anyone who comes into contact with Bill Shankly comes out a better person. You mightn't like him, you might think he's a bloody nuisance, but I'm grateful for all he taught me.' Today Tommy's admiration for Shankly has grown stronger with each passing year and he never tires of talking about the man.

Particularly prevalent in the memories of Shankly's former players is the kindness and concern that their former boss showed to the Liverpool fans. At away games, he'd tell his team, as they drove through the fans near the ground, 'See them, boys, don't let them down. Some of them can't afford it, yet they're still here to support you.'

Ray Clemence described the occasions when Shankly would bail out Reds fans who'd arrived in London with no train tickets, 'We used to go down on the train to play London sides. One or two Scousers would get on the train and not buy tickets. Invariably they'd get caught at the other end. Shanks, on many occasions, would go up to the ticket master and pay for those fans. They were in trouble, but he'd go and pay for them to get them out of trouble.'

Bill Shankly with his wife Nessie after receiving the OBE in 1974.

Fans also recalled Shankly's concern for their fellow Liverpool supporters, one Liverpool fan saying of a mid-1960s away game at Southampton, 'I watched as the Liverpool team coach pulled up outside the ground. As the players stepped off the coach and made their way into the players' entrance, Shanks walked over to a couple of Liverpool kids and asked them if they had had something to eat. He then took out his wallet and gave them a few pound notes. "Don't let me down, boys. Straight over to that cafe and get yourselves a nice warm meal," he told them. I watched as they immediately obeyed his orders. Gestures such as this were typical of the man.'

* * *

The idea that Bill Shankly, however, was some kind of saintly figure who never upset people would be totally misleading. Numerous football journalists,

as well as Shankly's players, would often find themselves on the receiving end of a tongue-lashing from the idiosyncratic Scot if he thought they deserved it.

Colin Wood of the *Daily Mail* once said, 'Working with Shankly was often like treading through a minefield. One false step and the explosion could blow you into little pieces. But then the warmth, the quick smile that told you that you were forgiven, and the invitation to a cup of tea put you back together again.' Wood claimed that Shankly only ever held a grudge against one reporter, the journalist who left Wembley during extra-time and missed Liverpool's famous victory over Leeds in the 1965 F A Cup final. That was sacrilege to Shankly.

In general, he didn't bear a grudge against any of his players who dared to argue with him either. He once admitted that he didn't care if a player didn't

Shankly shakes hands with the man he described as 'one of the greatest goalkeepers of all time', Ray Clemence, before his benefit match in 1975.

Bill Shankly salutes the
fans at Wembly in 1965.

like him, 'I deal with everybody as I think fit. Whether they like it or whether they don't, doesn't make any difference to me.'

Some at Anfield didn't appreciate Shankly's style, particularly during his early days there. Former international footballer and later a sports journalist, Ivor Broadis, once remarked, 'I remember someone at Liverpool saying Bill could be an awkward bugger. This other chap replied, "Aye, if Bill wasn't an awkward bugger, we'd still be in the Second Division."'

Shankly could certainly be scathing at times, particularly if any of his players reported themselves injured. 'Get that poof bandage off your leg,' he's alleged to have told one of his team who turned up at Melwood with his leg strapped up. 'But Boss, my leg ...' 'Your leg!' Shankly exploded, 'Your leg! That's Liverpool's leg. What do you mean, your leg!'

Injured players would quite often be sent to Coventry by Shankly. Once the injury had cleared up, Shankly would pass the time of day again with them. Tommy Smith once said that the way you were treated by Shankly when injured was quite comical. 'You would be lying on the treatment table and Bob Paisley might be giving you some treatment. Shankly would come in and ignore you, but say to Bob, "How is Smithy's leg?" I'd reply, "Tell Mr Shankly that Smith's leg isn't too good." Still ignoring me, Shanks would say, "Will he be fit for Saturday?" Bob would convey the question to me and I'd say, "Tell Mr Shankly that Smith doesn't know yet." This is the way it would carry on, with Shanks not asking me a direct question but talking through Bob.'

An injured player was no use to Liverpool Football Club, and right from the start Shankly expected his players to be as fanatical as him in their desire to take Liverpool to the top. He was known to have contacted golf clubs on Merseyside to check if any of his players were disobeying his request that they shouldn't participate in the sport. In Shankly's opinion, golf wasn't beneficial to certain parts of

'I do think that Bill would sometimes think about things and rehearse what he was going to say. I'm confident that some of his mannerisms were practised in front of a mirror. I don't think it was all totally off-the-cuff.'

Peter Robinson, Liverpool chief executive

the human anatomy. And it was the same when it came to alcohol. Shankly didn't mind his players having the odd beer, but if they overstepped the mark he would come down hard on them. 'Every player that comes here from the first day is being watched. We read them like a book. If he thinks that nobody is watching him, he's got a surprise coming,' Shankly once declared. On one famous occasion, Shankly is reputed to have entered a Liverpool city-centre club and dragged a player out by his hair, after the Liverpool manager had received reports that the player had been overdoing his night-clubbing activities.

* * *

Bill Shankly was undoubtedly totally selfless in his determination to turn Liverpool into a great club. Bob Paisley once said, 'One man transformed Liverpool from a run-of-the-mill Second Division team into the greatest club in the world. That man, of course, was Bill Shankly. His philosophy was simple: If you are going to play football, you play to win. While he was the making of Liverpool, there is no doubt that Anfield was the making of Bill Shankly. His character, his own enthusiasm, his will to win were so infectious.'

When asked what made Shankly so special as a manager, many of his former players cite his incredible ability to motivate them on the field of play: 'I was a big lad, but when the Boss finished with me, I felt even bigger. Having arrived from Scotland with a "will I make it?" feeling and perhaps lacking in confidence, Shanks made a fantastic difference to my game,' recalls former Liverpool skipper Ron Yeats. Alec Lindsay also felt the same about Shankly motivating him into becoming a better player, 'He got me working at my game, at my fitness, and he worked on my confidence. I was tried at left-back and never looked back'.

F A Cup final hero, Gerry Byrne, was actually on the transfer list when Shankly arrived at the club: 'I was in the reserves and seriously thinking about leaving when there was a change in manager and Bill Shankly came. Bill had confidence in me and I always tried never to let him down. That's one of the reasons why I was determined to stay on in the FA Cup final at Wembley. I would have done it just for him.'

Player after player expresses the same sentiments about Shankly's motivational abilities. Soccer legend, Sir Tom Finney, also noted that Shankly, Finney's former team-mate at Preston, was an expert at getting the best out of players. 'He got ordinary players performing beyond their capabilities, making them believe that they were better than even they thought.'

Shankly himself, however, believed that simply putting on the red shirt of Liverpool was enough motivation in itself. 'Fire in your belly comes from pride and passion in wearing the red shirt,' he would often proclaim. During the Shankly era, just the first sight of Anfield from their team coach would often strike the fear of God into most opposition players. 'We don't need to motivate players,' Shankly said, 'because each of them is responsible for the performance of the team as a whole. We aren't expecting a player to win a game by himself. We share out the worries. The status of Liverpool's players keeps them motivated.'

* * *

Liverpool's ability to 'share out the worries' as Shankly described it, enabled him to build two great teams, even though the teams weren't each comprised of eleven outstanding players. The players who weren't considered to be top-notch got by because of the great players in their team. Shankly, though he would be loathe to admit it – each of his players being described by him as the best player in that position in the world – did have his share of ordinary players. But within the framework of the Liverpool team they became competent units that gelled together into a very effective whole.

Many of Shankly's players never really were a success when tried at international level but were outstanding when representing Liverpool. The Leeds, Manchester United and Celtic teams of the 1960s also had their share of competent but not outstanding players. Yet all of these teams, like Shankly's Liverpool, achieved much success.

Perhaps if Shankly could have been persuaded to give up his beloved Liverpool and take over a Scotland team, which could boast such outstanding world-class players as Law, Bremner, Baxter and Mackey, with his phenomenal powers of motivation, they, and not England, might have been the first British side to win a World Cup.

'He mayn't have had any degrees in psychology, but he was the best brain-waster I've ever encountered – he used to make the players feel like giants, and opponents almost like pygmies!' declared Bob Paisley when asked about Shankly's ability to psyche his team up before a game.

* * *

Towards the end of 1997, a bronze figure of Bill Shankly in Messianic pose, standing ten feet tall, was unveiled at Anfield. The statue stands in the shadow of the Kop and is made from red Scottish granite. Many of his former players were present for the ceremony. Shankly's great friend and former team-mate, Tommy Docherty, told waiting reporters, 'Bill Shankly was fantastic, a great man and a great character and a man very much of the people. He'll never be forgotten anywhere in the world, but especially at Anfield where they absolutely idolise him. Shankly thought just as much of the supporters as well. They are fantastic supporters.'

The inscription on the base of the statue says simply 'Bill Shankly 1913-1981 – He Made the People Happy'.

The honour of unveiling the statue was given to Shankly's captain from the 1960s, Ron Yeats, who had once said of Shankly, 'He took Liverpool from nothing, and perhaps more difficult, he kept the club on the rails. A lot of clubs come up but they don't manage to keep it going. Bill Shankly laid the foundations right, and he made sure everyone at Anfield knew how to carry it on.'

Perhaps the most fitting tribute to Shankly came from one of Shankly's beloved Anfield faithful when he said, 'Bill Shankly gave his life to Liverpool Football Club. He never made much money from the game, but he died a much richer man than some of the second-rate managers who now reside in country mansions will ever be.'

BILL SHANKLY

He made the people happ

Liverpool sculptor Tom Murphy's bronze statue of Bill Shankly. Roger Hunt, Tommy Lawrence, Chris Lawler, Peter Thompson, Ron Yeats, Willie Stevenson, Ian Callaghan and Gerry Byrne, all members of the legendary team of the 1960s, at the unveiling of the Shankly statue in 1997. The presence of Shankly will loom large over Anfield for many years to come; as he once said, 'If you are first you are first. If you are second you are nothing.'

BIBLIOGRAPHY

Ian Callaghan and John Keith
The Ian Callaghan Story
Quartet Books, 1975

Steve Hale and Ivan Ponting
Liverpool in Europe
Guinness Publishing, 1992

Ian Hargraves, Ken Rogers and Ric George
Liverpool Club of the Century
Liverpool Echo Publication, 1988

Dean Hayes
100 Lancashire Footballing Greats 1946-1991
Didsbury Press, 1991

Steve Heighway
Liverpool My Team
Souvenir Press, 1977

Chris Nawrat and Steve Hutchings
*The Sunday Times Illustrated History
of Football, 1995*
Souvenir Press, 1977

Brian James
Journey to Wembley
Marshall Cavendish, 1977

Bob Paisley
Bob Paisley's Liverpool Scrapbook
Souvenir Press, 1979

Bob Paisley
My 50 Golden Reds
Front Page Books, 1990

Brian Pead
Liverpool a Complete Record 1892-1986
Breedon Books, 1986

Ivan Ponting
Liverpool Player by Player
Hamlyn, 1990

Ivan Ponting and Steve Hale
*Sir Roger – the Life and Times of Roger Hunt,
a Liverpool Legend*
Bluecoat Press 1995

Anton Rippon
The Story of Liverpool FC
Moorland Publishing, 1980

Gerald Sinstadt and Brian Barwick
*The Great Derbies: Everton v. Liverpool
A celebration of the Merseyside Derby*
BBC Books, 1988

Tommy Smith
I Did it the Hard Way
Arthur Barker, 1980

Phil Thompson
Do That Again Son and I'll Break Your Legs
Virgin Books, 1996

Phil Thompson
Shankly
Bluecoat Press, 1993

John Toshack
Tosh – An Autobiography
Arthur Barker, 1982